My Life As A Box Of Rocks

by

Mesa Morgan

authorHOUSE

1663 LIBERTY DRIVE, SUITE 200
BLOOMINGTON, INDIANA 47403
(800) 839-8640
www.authorhouse.com

First published by AuthorHouse 06/23/04

ISBN: 1-4184-0650-3 (sc)

Printed in the United States of America
Bloomington, Indiana

This book is printed on acid-free paper.

To the readers of this book: You have to realize that when I wrote this story, I was reliving, and feeling the moments of the past. It is written in the same manner that I speak; however I don't use profanity anymore. It would be demeaning, degrading, and unacceptable, however the passion is the very same passion that I felt when I was tripping along the road of life.

When a child comes into this world, it has to depend upon its parents, or other adults to take care of them. To love, care, feed them, and keep them from harm. Think about it. It is very scary, to have your life in the hands of another human being. To know that you're every breath, your very life is in their hands. The same hands that will hold, and caress you, or beat the living hell out of you for little, or no reason.

There are those children that are fortunate, and born into loving, caring families, and then there are those, that are just born. Those that are left to fend for themselves in the best way that they can, they are survivors. I was one of these children, and if there is such a thing as reincarnation, I don't want to come back as a human being, but as an eagle, or even a pine tree, but not as a human.

Sex, some, murder, almost, lies, not if I can help it, and scandals. It all depends on how you interpret what you read. However, this book is packed full of sixty years of confusion, excitement, a little love, a bit of hate, many betrayals, pain, laughter, and sorrows, and all the things that make life worth living, and some things that made me wish at times, that I was never born.

I wrote this book in hopes that someone would benefit from my experiences, and not make the horrible mistakes, and decisions that I had made. I was not lucky enough to have someone to guide me, or even to lead me in the right direction. I was like tumbleweed, for 63 years, gathering life as I rolled along. And the only thing I gathered was two husbands, several lovers, bills, and a ton of problems.   I also gathered eight children, several grandchildren, and two great grandchildren. All of this is in my story.

When I started to write this book, I was going to call it," Longing For Avonlea". However, once I started to write I realized that it had nothing at all to do with Avonlea, and everything to do with stupidity on a grand scale, and Avonlea was just a fictional place embedded in my heart. And then I finally settled on, " My Life As A Box of Rocks " which describes the majority of my life.

When I look back over the past 62 years I have come to realize that any man that was in my life was just there to take what I had to give. Except for my first love.   There was never real love or intimacy, (in-to-me-see) with any one else after my first fiancée broke our engagement. Finally, at age fifty-nine, I learned about the meaning of the *word intimacy in my Criminal Justice class, and knew then, I had never really experienced it. There was never any real communication between men and me. I always had to be a mind reader. My husband of thirty years usually answers any questions I ask with a grunt. I have to interpret the grunt to figure out the reply. I would like to tell my female readers, especially the younger ones, please...think, think, think, and don't be as "dumb as a box of rocks." Know in your heart that what you are doing is really what you want for yourself, and don't be duped or swayed by sweet talk, or crocodile tears, into changing your plans. My grandmother once said, "that a man will promise you the world with a gold fence around it to get his way." I think I was only ten when I heard it, and didn't have a clue. "What gold fence? Where?"*

This is my story, and I hope that you will take it to heart, and understand that all, and any decisions you make will forever alter your life, and determine whether you will be happy or miserable. If you have any doubts about your career, your feelings, marriage, find some one to talk to, AND LISTEN. Divorce was the option I chose with my first, husband, but with number two, it wasn't because I didn't want to be a serial divorcée and so with that decision, I decided to stick it out no matter how miserable I was. It was one of the worst mistakes I have ever made in a life where I had already made so many, and still today, I am married to my second mistake. So now, settle back, put your feet up and get ready to take a wild ride on my roller coaster of life.

Well, here it is the year 2000, and I survived the leap from one century to another, at our local gambling casino, and walked out fifteen dollars richer. I was hoping to win thousands, but my lady luck was still lost, back in 1999. Today is the same as yesterday, but I am a day older and a day wiser. Yeah...right.

I was hoping for a little excitement at the turn of the century, perhaps my utility company had lost my bill to the Y2K bug, or the power would have gone out, sending me running for my oil lamps, plunging me far back in time. But, no, I awake and everything is still up and running, including my automatic washer, which just went into the spin cycle. What a way to start the new Millennium! It is like every other day. A re-run! Today is the second day of the year 2000, and what a bummer! It is dark, dreary, and raining. I didn't want to get out of bed, but my old bones wouldn't allow me the pleasure of sleeping in. I lay there for a while, my mind spinning with things to write about, and where to start, until I got a wake up call from my bladder. When you get to be my age, you get several calls all night long, and sometimes I don't want to answer, but it's, get up, or wet the bed.

The idea for this book has been kicking around in my head for forty years. When I was twenty-two I had a landlady that I used to visit from time to *time. We would sit and talk. I told her about my life and what had taken place in my short time on this planet. She found my story to be exciting and very interesting and suggested that I write a book. Well, at twenty-two that was the last thing I wanted to do. I had a husband, and two babies to take care of, and not a brain in my head, with no clue as to what my future had in store for me. Now, forty years later, eight children, eight grandchildren, one great grand-daughter, two husbands, and a bad back, I finally have time to put together the wild tapestry of my life.*

I don't know where to start, so I will begin with my uneventful birth. Hell! I don't know if I was Monday's Child or Friday's Child, but after age five, I was no one's child, and had one brother and one sister. I will acquire another brother, and sister later on.

My father was sixty years old when I was born, and I think my mother was twenty-two. The story was that my father was a stowaway on a banana boat. He came to The United States from Italy. His parents came here first and left him behind. I think it was because he was incorrigible, or just plain bad. As a child I had heard that he knew Al Capone who had been a gangster. Whether that was true or not, I don't know. That is all I know about his entry into this country. He changed his name, and managed to become a welder, and at some point in time, met my mother. She became pregnant for me, and didn't get married until she was six months along. I don't think he was too happy about the turn of events that his life had taken, as I felt that he didn't like me. I also had a brother Joe and a sister Kate. I could tell right off the bat, that he adored my brother. My sister was too little for me to form an opinion about his feelings for her, as she wasn't old enough to talk or walk. I have a vague memory of my father trying to smother me with a pillow, and my grandmother stopping him. He never touched me again. This was my first memory of her, and I knew then, that she did not like my father. I didn't see her again until well after he had died from pneumonia.

From what I can recall, my father was a good provider. He was a welder by trade. We lived in a cute little cottage right next door to where he worked, and we had a car, a model T Ford.

I have a few warm memories that stick in my mind like super glue, and they are warm ones. Some mornings at about 5am I would hear the clippity clop of the horses pulling the milk wagon that delivered the milk. It was just before they started to use trucks for deliveries. I also remember a man with a horse drawn wagon that used to call out for rags, and people would bring out their old worn out clothing and sell it to him, and there was a man that sold vegetables, and fruit from the back of an old truck. He had converted it to accommodate shelves, and it had a fabric top of some kind to keep the rain off the produce.

Life seemed to be normal from my four and five year old eyes. But what did I know? We visited my grandparents, who spoke no English, and scared me half to death because they didn't. My father's family was large and he had several brothers and two sisters. They all owned land together out in the country somewhere, and they all had produce gardens. Sometimes we would go there in the summer. After my father died we didn't see his family anymore. I had the feeling that they didn't like my mother and resented the fact that my father had married a non-Italian. The odd part of my years with both parents is the fact that I don't recall my mother. I remember a sitter, but my mother didn't work. I didn't really see that much of her until after my father died, and then the fat hit the fan!

It was 1946, and World War Two was over. Shirley Temple was hot at the box office, and there were soldiers and sailors all over the place. It seemed a lot of them were at my house, along with women that I had never seen before, except for an aunt that had left her husband to join the parties that my mother had. I was a cute kid, and could sing and dance like Shirley Temple, I even had curly hair like hers. When they wanted to get rid of me, they would ask me to dance and then give me money so I would go to bed. I do remember that it was noisy and there was a lot of drinking and laughter, and then the bomb dropped!

The bomb came in the form of my mother's mother. My grandmother, and she was a force to be reckoned with! It seemed that someone went to her house to complain about the wild parties that her daughter was having. There weren't too many telephones back then, so they weren't able to call. They had to go in person. My grandmother came storming in, and people went flying out! The police showed up looking for my aunt. My grandmother gave them the what for, and routed out my aunt, sending her back home to her husband. Things became quiet after that. My mother would leave us and go to the local bar. One night a female detective came to our house and found us alone. With a little bribery of candy she managed to get me to tell where our mother was. The next thing I knew, we were moving in with my grandmother, and to my surprise, I find that I have an older brother.

Picture this, a widow, with a two-bedroom apartment and a closet with a toilet in it, and one boy. Her family has now grown from one child, to four, and, again, I don't recall my mother being there. Now that I think of it, she couldn't have been. My grandmother slept in the other bedroom. She introduced Bill to us. He is our brother. We accept him, but are too young to know why he is our brother.

It was warm, clean and comfortable. We kids all shared one bedroom, and two beds, the boy's in one bed, and we girls in the other. Bedtime was always mayhem because we always raised hell before we finally went to sleep, but it was fun. My gram had to make several trips to our room to make us quiet down.

There was no central heating. We had a pot-bellied stove in the dining room and that was it. We took our baths once a week in a galvanized tub with water that had been heated on the potbelly, and gas stove. My gram took care of the stove and kept it fed with wood and coal. Many winter mornings I would awake to the sounds of her shaking down the ashes to get it roaring hot before we got out of bed. The bedrooms were really cold in the winter, and sometimes we would wet the bed because I think we didn't want to come out from beneath the warm blankets. It was so cold that the windows would ice over inside from the condensation. We would scratch pictures in the panes with our fingers, and found this to be a great form of entertainment.

The kitchen was kept warm by my grandmothers cooking and baking. I can still remember the smell of warm bread baking when I came in from school, but hated the fact that I would have to clean the bread bowls and pans that were used for the making and baking. By the time I got home, the dough had hardened on, and they were hard to clean. At eight years old I was learning to bake, clean house, and baby-sit. My first batch of biscuits were like hockey pucks. The only way you could eat them was by dunking them in coffee. Yes, my gram let us have coffee, but it had a lot of milk in it. Sometimes we had Ovaltine, or even tea.

The woman upstairs had a baby, and when she and her husband went out they would ask my gram if I could baby-sit. My gram let me, because she was right down stairs. I remember when the baby was born. It was at night, and I had been asleep. I was awakened by screams coming from upstairs, and there was a flurry of activity by my gram. I sneaked out of bed, and was peeking in the hallway. I saw them taking bloody rags to the trashcan, and couldn't imagine what had happened. It was very scary seeing all that blood, and Yuk. The next thing I knew, there was a new baby.

Gram always made sure that Christmas was wonderful. I don't know how she did it, but they are my favorite memories. The smells, the sounds, the food, and the toys, and the five-pointed red star that lit up the front window to signal the coming of Christmas. It was so exciting! After Christmas, my brother Bill and I would go around and drag some old Christmas trees back to our house and build a fort in the snow. Sometimes we would even find an ornament that someone had forgotten. It was like finding hidden treasure! And then came Easter, a time for new clothes, shoes, and Easter Bonnets. The shoes were black patent leather with a black bow on the top. I remember wearing my new shoes to bed because I was afraid that someone might sneak in and take them while I was sleeping. I can't imagine why I would have thoughts like that.

My grandmother would never let us out of her sight. In the summer time when we played, it was in the front of the house. She would sit on the porch and watch us. We played games like, Red Rover, Red Rover, Hop Scotch, The Pie Man, and jumped rope. We were not allowed to go to anyone's home, and we didn't have friend's over. In the summer when it was hot, our swimming pool was at the side of the curb when it was raining. My brother Bill and I made scooters from orange crates, a two by four, and a roller skate, but we could only ride them as far as my gram could see. In the winter we would sleigh ride, or stay in the house, and play cards, and Monopoly, or listen to stories on the radio while we munched on home made popcorn and fudge.

In the beginning life was pretty good by my standards, until my father's insurance money ran out. I would never know comfort again. I learned about poverty and pain, and welfare, which I didn't understand at the time. I learned to survive, and make do with what we had, and to earn some of the things we didn't have.

At ten years old I was chopping wood, and carrying buckets of coal, and one time I even had to chop the head off a chicken for dinner. Kate remembers watching the chicken take a few steps with no head. That was creepy! We earned most of our money by shoveling sidewalks in the winter and taking out ashes. This was the residue left behind by burning coal for heat. Sometimes we would sprinkle it on sidewalks to keep people from slipping when they walked. In the summer we would run errands, and sell ice. Back then the local dairy barn, (that is what it was called), used chunks of ice to keep the milk cold for delivery. The reason it was called a dairy barn is because before delivery trucks, the milk was delivered by horse drawn wagons, and they still had the barn. At the end of the day, my older brother and I would take our red wagon, go to the dairy barn, and pick up the left over ice. We would go door to door and sell it to people who had iceboxes. (There weren't too many people in our neighborhood that owned refrigerators at the time). We would charge by the size of the chunk, five or ten cents. It wasn't a bad little enterprise and it helped keep food on the table. Bill and I would also collect old newspapers and cardboard and take them to the junkyard. Cardboard always paid more. That little red wagon made us a lot of money. When business petered out, we found other ways of earning money. We started stealing milk bottles off people's back porches and turning them in for the refund. The little red wagon became a way to haul stolen toys, and the bottles. Of course, my grandmother never found this out. She would have killed us!

I remember the time my brother Bill and I wanted to give our gram some flowers for Mother's Day. We didn't have any money so we scouted the neighborhood until we found a blooming plant of flowers on someone's porch. We gave them to her, and she was so happy to get them. She put them right in the front window where the whole world would see them. I was a nervous wreck until the plants died, and she took them out of the window. I don't know what would have happened to us if she ever knew how we really got them. Bill and I would probably be pushing up our own flowers, because she would have beaten us to death.

She never suspected that we were little criminals. Any money we had, she figured we worked for, because for the most part, any money we made went into food for the house. When I say food, I mean, bread, milk, oleo, and peanut butter. We didn't have bottled milk, but mixed evaporated milk with water.

My gram had wealthy in-laws and once in awhile they would drive up in their black Cadillac Sedan. They dropped off used clothing, and I think they gave my gram some money. They would give us money that we would put in our little Fido dog banks. They would tell us that if we left it there, the next time they came, they would double it. Needless to say, it never even made it to the bank. As soon as they cleared the curb we went running down the street to the ice cream store. After awhile they stopped coming. I don't remember why.

We all went to Catholic School, even though my gram wasn't Catholic. We had to walk at least a mile, even in a snowstorm. At the time, and being very little, it seemed more like five miles. Alone, the walk would have been frightening, but with my brother Bill, it was fun. It was even better when Kate and Joe started going.

I was sure that when I grew up, I was going to be a Nun. I loved all the pomp, and ceremony. I also noticed that the sisters ate very well, and wanted for nothing. I even enjoyed going to church on Sunday. I managed to make my First Communion, and Confirmation. As I grew older I noticed that the Nuns were both brutal, and kind. Because we were poor, the Nuns would take us down into the basement of the school and pick out clothes for us to wear. They were clothes that were donated for the needy. Once in a while some kid would poke fun at me because the clothes were too big. I developed a thick skin and wouldn't let it bother me.

This may gross you out, but because we didn't have a lot of candy, or money to buy any, I would sometimes pick up gum from the schoolyard and chew it. It still had the sugar in it because the kid's had to spit it out when the bell rang and we had to go back inside after playtime. I would chew it like crazy, and then swallow it so that I wouldn't get caught with it in my mouth. I really don't think anyone ever saw me do it, and I can't believe that I did that, but I did.

It is a wonder that I didn't contract some kind of a disease!

I was always looking on the ground for money. One time I saw a quarter beneath a grate next to the corner store on my way home from school. I tried every trick in the book to get it, but to no avail. I think I lay on my stomach on the ground for more than an hour trying to get that elusive coin.

I was excellent at spelling and would win little awards. They were always pictures or medals of Jesus, The Blessed Mother, or saints. When it came to math, I just couldn't get it, so I got the pointer across the knuckles instead.

Things at home were going downhill fast. My mother showed up. From where, I have no idea. Gram moved her bed into the living room and my mother had my gram's bedroom. She was there for a short time, and then left again. Bill got her room. Things kept getting worse. My gram couldn't stand my little brother Joe because he reminded her of my father. Soon he began to irritate the hell out of her and he did things that would cause her to beat him. She would even tie him to a chair in the kitchen, and put cayenne pepper in his mouth. I would watch from my bedroom doorway, as he screamed and cried. When she could no longer stand to hear him, she would tie a gag in his mouth. I wanted to help him so bad, but I couldn't, out of fear for what might happen to me if I did. My sister Kate was in the bedroom behind me. She was scared half to death. This was a living nightmare. To escape, I delved into the world of books and became an avid reader.

The first book I ever read was Heidi. I fell in love with the story and wanted to be like her and live in the mountains. My next book was Little Women, followed by, Little Men. I soon discovered a line of biographies written by Louisa May Alcott for children my age, and I read them all. The more I read, the more I wanted to read. I became obsessed. I found a whole new world, and a place to hide, where everything was wonderful, and exciting. I could go to places I had never dreamed of. I became a part of the story. In my mind, I was there. However, reality was always pounding at the door, and I would have to answer it sooner or later.

Once again, my mother returns. She has a little baby with her. Her name is Edith. She is our new sister. We know nothing about how she got there. She is just there. My grandmother adored her and found great pleasure in her presence. My mother had a nervous breakdown, and my grandmother put her away in a place we called the nut house. Now, there are five mouths to feed and never enough food.

When I went to church on Sunday, I no longer paid attention to the mass, but spent my time listening for the sound of money falling on the floor when the collection basket was passed. I would memorize where I heard it fall, and then after school on

Monday I would go into the church to look for the change on the floor. I became bolder. I was now going up to the votive holder, which was overflowing with change. It was jammed up in the slot, and I helped myself. No one saw me, except God. He knew I needed it. I don't think he cared.

One Monday after school I was making my rounds in the church, and I found a wallet. I didn't look inside, and I didn't keep it. The thought scared me half to death, so I went running back to school with it and gave it to a Nun. Go figure. My perception of right and wrong was twisted. It had to be.

Sometimes during the summer when it was really hot, my gram would make us go in the house and take a nap. She would pull the shades, and darken the rooms, and we were to lie down and be quiet, and hopefully, for her sake, fall asleep. I think she did this because she needed a break. One day when we were supposed to be napping, I decided to heat water and mop the kitchen floor, as this was a part of my chores. While pouring the boiling hot water in the mop pail, Edith came up behind me and yelled. I dropped the pan of boiling hot water, slipped, fell, and scalded my tuckus on the left side. I also scalded the inside of my right ankle. I was screaming like a Banshee and everyone came running. My ankle bubbled, and so did my tuckus. My gram put Vaseline on it, and covered it with an old diaper. I never did finish mopping the floor.

Things were getting worse, and I was getting older. I began to realize there is more to life than what I was experiencing, I was learning this from reading, but my first awakening came when I was invited to a birthday party. It was the first time anyone ever asked me to one. I asked my gram if I could go. She said no. I asked why. She told me I was not to question why, but to do as she said. I was determined to go. I had a plan. I told my brother Bill about the party. He told me to meet him down by the corner market when the party was over. We would go home together, and tell gram that I went with him to help sell papers. I was so excited! My first party! I had no gift and no money to buy one, so I took the oval picture of The Blessed Mother off the wall and that was my gift. I had won it in a spelling contest at school, and had given it to my gram. I put on a pink dress, and put the picture in my pocket. The dress had a tear in it, but I was too happy to care. I went to my girlfriend's house so we could go to the party together. Her mom noticed the tear in my dress and mended it. Soon we were on our way to have a good time. I was on cloud nine! What a surprise! She lived in a big beautiful house! She had her own bedroom, and beautiful clothes. We played games, and had cake and ice cream, and then the party was over. I hurried to meet my brother. He wasn't there. I waited for a while, but got scared because it was getting dark. I decided to go home and wing it. I went up on the porch. I noticed that the power is off again and the oil lamps were burning, and then I saw my brother Bill standing next to my grandmother! I was in deep doo-doo! With no plan, I walked in as if everything was all right. Gram asked me where I had been. I stayed with the plan, and told her that I was with Bill selling newspapers. He stepped out from behind her and told her that I wasn't with him. To add insult to injury, he held me down across her bed so she could whip my tuckus with a razor strop. The whippings were becoming more frequent as I became bolder, and I was getting tired of it. I spent a lot of time thinking about how I could get away from this hellhole of a life. I knew that somewhere, there was something better. This was the beginning of a whole new adventure and I started to run away from home.

At that time Roy Rogers and Dale Evans were big Movie Stars. They were adopting kids. I got the idea that maybe I could get them to adopt me! I wrote a letter to Roy and Dale and asked them if they would. I don't have to tell you. They didn't. They just sent me an autographed picture of themselves with their horse Trigger. I was so disappointed. I thought for sure that they would. This, was when I first decided to leave home, I was going out west! I was going to try and find Roy and Dale. Maybe if they saw me they would like me enough to adopt me. After all, I was a cute kid, and talented too! Without saying anything to anyone, I took off. I kept my eyes on the sun. I knew it set in the west, and I kept walking in that direction. Many hours later, I approached what was known as Boomer Hill. There were no streetlights, and it was getting dark. I was losing my bravado with the setting sun and I was sure there were monsters lurking in the darkness to grab and eat me. I was terrified. I whistled, and sang to ease my fear. It's funny, but as I write this, I can recall that whenever I whistled around my grandmother she would always say, "that whistling girls, and cackling hens, will always come to some bad ends". And you know what? She was right. It seemed like the more I whistled, the more trouble I got into. The trouble started out small, but would eventually balloon into bigger trouble. Why, you would think that I had been whistling with the power of a train whistle! Anyway, I turned around and headed back down that long highway towards home. After walking for what seemed like forever, a police car stopped and picked me up. I didn't know if he was looking for me or not, but he took me home. I told him that I was afraid that my gram would beat me. When we went into the hallway, he put me behind him, and then knocked on the door. My gram answered. She was hopping mad! The policeman told her that she wasn't to hit me, and then he left. She didn't touch me, but she ranted and raved about how ungrateful I was.

Gram was beginning to have heart problems. We were just too much for her to handle. Her temper was getting shorter and shorter. One day she accused my brother Bill of stealing $20.00 from her. That was a lot of money! They were yelling at each other. Then she popped him in the face, and called him a French Bastard! I didn't even know what the word *meant, but it sure sounded awful! I was in shock! I thought he was the same as us! Then it became known that he was only my half brother. It seems that my mother became pregnant for him when she was very young and unmarried. My grandmother adopted him legally and gave him her name, which I never gave a thought to. His last name was different than ours! And I never realized it! (The little box of rocks is beginning to grow.) To us, he was still our older brother, whole, or half.*

One day, Bill took Joe over to the dairy barn. Somehow they managed to get inside where the milk was bottled. They found some pink looking liquid in a bottle and thought it might be strawberry flavoring. Bill dared Joe to drink it. Joe did, and then they came home. The next thing I knew there was a police car in front of the house and my gram was yelling. It seemed that the pink stuff was poison, and Joe drank enough to kill ten men! My gram forced Joe to drink milk and raw eggs, and then they rushed him off to the hospital in the police car. I think they pumped his stomach. He was okay, and returned home, a hero. This was one time he didn't get a beating.

From what I gathered, my mother was an only child, and very spoiled. She had everything. An adoring father, a beautiful home, and all that went with it. He called her Princess, but her wonderful life came to an end when her dad had an automobile accident. He was sued for everything they owned except their personal belongings. At that time, automobiles were new, and there was no such thing as auto insurance. It was some time after that, her dad died from tuberculosis. I saw some of the remnants of her childhood in an old trunk. There was a lock of her hair in a blue velvet lined Mother of Pearl oyster shell with a gold clasp on it. There was also a little gold baby ring with rubies in it. It was on a blue velvet rod that fit inside of a silver cylinder. I remember a picture of my mother when she was a teenager. It was in a frame of pewter, her hair was dark, and worn in a pageboy style. Her dress had a v-neck, and gram said it was made of blue velvet. She looked like a rich kid. Gram also had a crystal vanity set that was supposed to hold powder and perfumes. You just knew that at one time, she had a great life, and now all she had was five kids and a bad heart. The fickle finger of fate sure has a way of coming into your life and screwing things up.

We were getting wilder all the time. Gone, were the summer evenings of playing games on the front porch, under the watchful eye of gram, and gone were the winter nights of sitting around the dining room table playing Monopoly, and listening to the radio. Now, we older ones were running amok, and taking the smaller ones with us. I particularly recall a time when I took off for the local park dragging my little brother along. My grandmother found us there wandering around in the dark. I got the switch to my rear end, and promised to never do that again. I didn't, do that particular thing again, but I found more exciting things to do, and my tuckus paid the price.

While digging through people's trash one day, I found an old car battery. I took it to the junkyard and got five dollars for it. Boy! I was rich! At least I felt like I was. I told Bill about my great fortune. He suggested that we go and buy BBs, and candy. We did. Bill and I took slingshots, the BBs and went down to the railroad yard and shot at each other. We would hide behind the trains and use them as shields. How we ever missed putting an eye out was beyond me. One day we even went downtown to ride the escalators in the five and dime store. The store detective tried to get us to leave. He said we could have anything we wanted if we would go home. I told Bill to ask for a bike. It didn't work, so we settled for a pound of licorice babies. Sometimes I would skip school and go to the zoo... and things at home are getting bad.

My little brother Joe was always getting into trouble. He had a fight with a neighbor boy, and whacked the kid in the arm with a hammer. The boy's mother came over screaming saying "if her son gets cancer" she will sue! I didn't have a clue about cancer or sue. All I know is Joe took another beating from gram. Joe, in his frustration, put his fist through the glass in the kitchen door. He cut his fist and there was blood all over. The next thing I know, Joe is gone, forever. A few weeks later, Bill is gone too. They were sent to a foster home. I had no conception of the words, and just accepted the fact that they were gone. I was hoping for the best where my little brother Joe was concerned. Maybe he would have a better life. It was not to be, as I would find out later.

My Grandmother's health is getting worse, and it is difficult for her to take care of us. We go to school raggedy. We even had head lice. That was horrible, as gram used kerosene, and a little metal comb to get rid of them. Cockroaches moved in and took up residency with us, and our dog was dumping and wetting on the kitchen floor. It became my job to clean it up. This was all very nasty to me, and I didn't like it. I knew in my heart that this was no way to be living but couldn't do anything about it.

There was no cafeteria that fixed lunches at school, but you could bring one in a bag and eat it in a room they called a lunchroom, however the milkman delivered crates of milk to the school every day. We would usually go home for lunch. I didn't want to do this anymore. I wanted to stay at school and eat. We didn't have the makings for sandwiches, so I would make one, using mustard and sugar. Once in awhile, if I were lucky, I would have a little bottle of white milk. I wanted chocolate so bad, but couldn't get it. That was a luxury. The kid's made fun of me, and staying at school for lunch didn't last long. I am not a happy kid. I am older, and getting bolder.

It was brought to my attention that there was something coming to town, called The State Fair. There was a boy in school that was going to be working there. He liked me, and told me that I could go on the ride where he would be working, for free. I am really excited! I tell my Sister Kate. (Now, mind you, I am only eleven years old, but look older as I have developed boobs, and she is only six or seven). The next day, we skipped school and went to The Fair. I don't recall paying to get in, as I had no money, but I do remember how exciting it all was. The ride was The Caterpillar. There was a top that would cover over you as the ride went around in a large circle on a track. The boy from school that operated the ride took a break and rode with Kate and I, once. He was kissing me, and I remember that I didn't like it, and wondered why he did. Boy! Was I stupid! (There is that growing box of rocks again.) It was getting dark, so I decided that we should leave and go home. Knowing that I was going to get a beating, I decided not to go straight home. Kate and I went over to the Italian bakery and stood outside looking in the window just drooling and enjoying the smell of fresh bread baking. We were very hungry, as we had not eaten all day. Now, it is very dark out, and late, so we headed home. When we arrived home, I got my beating, and Kate just got yelled at, because I was the one that dragged her along. I didn't mind the beating because it was a small price to pay for adventure, and we were used to it, my tuckus and me.

My grandmother could no longer control me. The next thing I knew, she was asking me if I wanted to go live with Angie on the river. Angie was the woman who had lived upstairs over us, and had the baby. She had moved and had another kid. I said okay, because I liked Angie, and this would be a new adventure for me. Well, this turned out to be one hell of a nightmare. It seemed that she needed someone to help her with her kid's, and I was elected. Back in those days people used cloth diapers. When a baby took a dump, you would have to rinse the crap out before you could put them to soak. They didn't have a toilet there, only an outhouse. I had to take the crappy diapers down to the river and clean them out. This was a bitch because it was winter and my hands froze all the time. I got sick of helping her with her kids and decided that I wanted to get out of there. I found my way back to gram, but she sent me off to my first foster home. The only explanation for my departure was that my Gram was too sick to take care of me.

The foster home turned out to be a farm. What a surprise I had upon my arrival! My brothers were there too! I was happy! But, it would be short lived. The farm was a Dairy Farm. The man and woman that owned it were our foster parents. A substitute mother and father. There were thirty-six milking cows. There was no indoor bathroom but an outhouse. I was already familiar with that because Angie had one. There was only cold running water, and it was in the dining room, next to the kitchen.

It had a living room that was referred to as a parlor. We never spent any time there. There were two bedrooms in the whole house. One, downstairs, and one very large room upstairs, that I shared with my two brothers. The room was separated by what was called a dressing screen, and we had a commode, (a nice name for slop pot) that we would use during the night when we had to go pee. It was my job to empty the nasty thing in the morning before I went to the barn.

In the dining room on the wall was a crank telephone. You would have to turn the crank once to get the operator, and then have her connect to your party. You always knew when someone got a call. We were on a party line, and their calls would ring in our house. The people were recognized by the amount of rings on the phone, and you could eves-drop if you were nosey enough. If you needed to make a call you would just tell the operator that you wanted to talk to whomever, and she would ring them up.

It didn't take me long to figure out the reason we were really there. These people needed farm hands, and we were it. I was about eleven or twelve years old. My little brother Joe was around seven, and Bill was older than both of us.

I was soon introduced to the daily rigors of farm work. I didn't mind. In fact I found a special pride in being able to work like a man. My first duty of the day was getting up at four-thirty in the morning, emptying the commode, and getting dressed.   Then I would wake up my brothers and head down to the barn by 5am.

I had to get things started. I would switch on the barn lights, and the power would come on accompanied by the Radio Show, " The Wired Woodshed". We only had two milking machines. I would put them on the cows, and then my foster father would come down. After I removed a machine from a cow, I would have to strip her, meaning I would have to hand milk her for the remaining milk. My brothers would clean the trenches and feed the heifers and bulls. While they were busy at this, I would take the pails of milk across the barnyard to the milk house.   When the milking was finished I would pull the big cans of milk from the cooler and put them out for the milkman to pick up. These cans seemed to weigh a ton. The water in the cooler helped me to pull them up and get them out, Once this was accomplished I would take a ladle and scoop out a heaping ladle full of heavy cream from the top, and drink it. It was delicious! After this was done, I would head back up to the house and help get breakfast on the table. Soon my brothers came in, followed by the old man. We got cleaned up, ate, and then went out to get the school bus. I loved school. It wasn't Catholic, and it was fun. Soon, I would want to go to school seven days a week.

The old man started to become cranky. He didn't feel that we were working up to his expectations.

One morning down in the barn, he took a small whip and went after my little brother. It seems that Joe wasn't cleaning the trenches fast enough. Bill was in some other part of the barn, and didn't hear the fracas. I got pissed and went after the old man. He was flabbergasted. I got whacked once with the whip, but he didn't do it again. After that, he didn't like me, and would find an excuse to shove me from behind, especially when we would come into the house from the barn. There was a shed attached to the kitchen where we would leave our coats and boots. I always had to use a bootjack to get my boots off. While I was struggling to get them off he would push me and tell me to quit stalling. I was really beginning to hate this man. His wife wasn't too bad, but bad enough. She would make me cotton skirts to wear to school. If I didn't work fast enough to please her, or objected to too many chores, she would say," why do you think I made you those skirts"? I guess that was my payment for all the work I did.

One evening we were eating dinner. It was the usual fare of roast beef, vegetables and potatoes. I happened to take more mustard than I needed. I tried to shake it off my fork. The old man, told me to eat it. I said, no, I didn't want it. Once again he ordered me to eat it. Once again, I refused. My brothers had stopped eating and were watching. The old man got up from his chair and came over to me. He took the hand with the fork and mustard on it, and tried to shove it into my mouth. My head was bobbing and weaving to avoid the fork. He finally caught it in my hair, and pulled up. I got pissed. I got out of the chair and tried to pop him one in the head. We were bumping around the dining room pushing and shoving each other. His wife finally grabbed a broom and broke us up. My brothers did nothing. They looked like they were in shock. I had so much anger built up inside of me, that it didn't bother me to go up against a full grown man. All I know is that it felt good to be able to hit him back. The next day, I went to school and called the social worker that had brought me there. I told him what the old man did, and how he used the whip on us. Instead of them taking me out of there, they took my brothers. They sent them to another foster farm. I was now alone, and the only farm hand they had, and my workload increased. I still didn't mind it that much, but one day I had worked my ass off, and I was tired. The old man decided that he wanted me to shovel manure from the barnyard into the honey wagon. (manure spreader.) I was so pissed that I stood in the barnyard denouncing God. I just knew that he didn't exist. If he did, I wouldn't be a virtual slave. That was how I felt, but I still didn't mind busting my ass, but there had to be a limit. There wasn't. It was work, work, work, and no play. If I wasn't working in the barn, fields, or garden, I had to mend feedbags. I even drove the tractor when I was needed to. The farmer up in back, and over the hill, told the old man, that when I got older, I would pay for all that hard work. I didn't know what he meant.

At school I had a girlfriend. Her name was Susan. We became very close, and school was the best place to be. At lunch time the school would close off half the gym so we could play volleyball. I was on the honor roll and also had a part in a school play. Because my voice was loud and could carry across the auditorium, I played the villain. However, the turn of events later on, would keep me from my debut as an actress.

One day Susan asked me to spend the night at her house. I was so excited! As soon as I got home from school I asked my foster mother if I could. She said that she would see. I was hoping and praying. I really needed God's intervention this time. (I had forgotten that he didn't exist). I must have promised my life or something, because my prayers had been answered! I was going to spend the night! I got off the school bus at Susan's house. It wasn't a farm, even though it was in the country. Her mother was really nice, and there was no work to be done! It was like heaven! We stayed awake real late talking about everything. We even had popcorn and soda. This was so different from the way I lived. I never had soda pop, or popcorn, only milk, or water. It was the shortest night of my life, and would never happen again. One evening Susan went to a Donkey Basketball game with some friends of her family. They were driving back when something happened. Susan was killed. I couldn't believe it! I wanted to go to the funeral, but my foster mother said no, that it was no place for me to be. I think that she said that she would send flowers. I don't think she did. I never heard anything from Susan's mom. I don't even remember if I cried. Eventually I met another girl who would also become my good friend. Her name was Ann. She would soon play a different part in my life.

Life on the farm stayed pretty much the same except that after school I would have homemade cookies, and milk before I went to the barn to do my chores, and help with the milking. I worked my ass off as usual. At about the age of thirteen I got my period. No one had ever talked to me about this, and I was terrified when I found blood in my underpants. I didn't know what was happening. I went to my foster mother and told her what had happened. She gave me the story about becoming a young lady, (of course, I didn't act like a young lady, working like a man, and all), and told me to expect this every month for many, many years. She would make my menstrual pads from cotton and gauze. It was disgusting. I never knew that you could buy them in a store until I left there. For some reason, after that, I didn't like being around the old man. I sensed something had changed, and I had better be on my guard.

The old man had a nephew that would come to spend a week or two in the summer. He was lazy and didn't work near as hard as I did. I didn't like him. One day he was supposed to have put lime on the barn floor. He didn't. The old man came along and questioned why it had not been done. I told him that his nephew was supposed to do it. The nephew said I was supposed to do it. I got pissed, and jumped him. I was getting my licks in, while the old man stood there goading his nephew to get me. I won the fight. The old man wasn't happy, and neither was his nephew.

I still enjoyed the hard work, but was getting tired of having no fun. I started to complain. The old man started trying to use the whip on me again. He would catch me by surprise when my back was turned. I hated him. I decided to call my worker and blow him in. The next day I called my worker from school. He came out to the farm, and we talked outside before he went in the house. I showed him the whip. He left me outside and went in the house to talk with the old man and his wife. He came out and told me that it was okay, and they wouldn't beat me anymore. Like a dummy, I believe him. After he left, the old man called me to come in. I went in. I was standing at the sink washing my hands, when all of a sudden, whap, he slapped me up side my head so hard, my ears rang. I was super pissed, but I don't cry. I think he wanted me to, but I wouldn't, and I didn't. My gram taught me early on that there was nothing to be gained by shedding tears, real, or crocodile. When I did cry, which wasn't often, she would say, that my bladder was too close to my eyes. (At the time I had no clue about my bladder.) The next day I went to school and called my social worker again. I told him that if he didn't take me out of this home, I was going to run away. The next day he showed up and went into the house to talk with them. I wasn't waiting around for a repeat performance of the last time he was there. I left. Maybe an hour and a half later, my worker pulled up along side of me in his car. He told me to get in. I said no. I told him that I wasn't going back there. He said that he wasn't going to take me back. I got into his car. He took me to a place called the detention home. This was the reason I never got to be in the school play.

The detention home was in an old gray Victorian house. There were about five other girls there. Why they were there, I can't remember. They didn't seem to be bad, and we had fun. We slept in something called a dormitory. We all ate our meals at a large round dining room table. The woman that watched over us was very nice. She was very prim and proper, but not strict. She used to read me my future from the tealeaves in the bottom of the cup from my tea. I remember one of her readings. She said that she saw me moving around a lot. She was right. I liked her. She was different from any one I had ever known. I stayed there until another foster home was found for me to go to.

The foster people were not Catholic, but Protestants. They had a boy around my age. Right off the bat he started to pick on me about being a farmer. I popped him in the head putting an end to his crap, and any thoughts he may have had about pushing *me around. I could only stay for six months, after which I had to go to a Catholic home, even though I went to church every Sunday. I liked it there. My foster mother was terrific. My foster father was scary, but in looks and attitude only. He was a big man, balding with a belly. He had false teeth that he would pop in and out of his mouth. He never said much. I learned to like him though. We would watch the Friday night fights on television together, and have ice cream sodas. I think he worked in the steel mill. He was also a member of a local Volunteer Fire Department, and drove a fire truck.*

The Foster Home was also an emergency home. Sometimes, when babies or kids were left alone, the Police would bring them to our house in the middle of the night. I never knew how many kids were going to be there when I woke up in the morning. The boy that I popped was a permanent resident. He was as old as I, and had been with these people since he was a little baby. Many years later I learned that this jerk used to climb on the roof, and peek into my bedroom window, and watch me undress for bed. I never suspected a thing. He was lucky I never caught him. I would have maimed him for life.

My foster mother treated me like a daughter. We shared the housework and shopped together. She knew I smoked, (something I learned from the other kids at my new school), but didn't want me to smoke in front of her. She told me that if I ever needed money for cigarettes, to just take it out of her purse. The only thing she asked in return was that I tell her when I took it. Life was good, and I was beginning to feel like I belonged to a real family. Wrong again. After six months my Social Worker came to take me out of my wonderful home, and put me in a nice Catholic one. As far as I was concerned there was no such thing as a "nice" Catholic home.

To my surprise, he took me to the same home where my two sisters were. I don't remember if I was happy to see them or not. I must have been, as we are sisters. Kate filled me in on why they were there and told me what happened to gram. She just couldn't handle caring for them anymore because of her failing health. These foster parents were very young and had two small boys. And right off the bat I knew why we were there, to clean house, and baby-sit. I was right. All three of us were slaves. Their children would get real milk to drink while we had instant. They had real butter and we had oleo.

I began to rebel against their authority. I started to skip school. One of the girls at my new school told me about a cute guy she had met, and wanted me to go with her to his house. His name was Eric. I was game, and off we went. Had I but known that he was the major reason that my life would be so screwed up; I would have never gone to meet him. He was good looking. He reminded me a little of Marlon Brando, who was the latest movie star. Eric was about five feet ten. He had dark brown curly hair, brown eyes, and full lips with a great smile. He was wearing blue jeans, a plaid shirt with the sleeves rolled up, and engineer boots, and I could tell that he liked me. He asked me for my phone number, and I gave it to him. My girlfriend and I left. I arrived home to find out that the school had called and wanted to know why I wasn't there. My foster mother was really pissed and grilled me as to my whereabouts that day. I didn't tell her about Eric, and she never found out about him. I would only talk to him when they weren't home. Eric felt sorry for me and wanted his mother to adopt me. He asked her to, and she explained why she couldn't. I wasn't sure I wanted to be adopted by anyone. I wasn't a baby anymore. I was all grown up. I thought.

I didn't even spend a year in this foster home. I ran away with the help of Eric. He pitched a tent in the woods not too far away from where he lived. This spot was only accessible by going hand over hand over some heavy utility wire. It was on a hill surrounded by a small creek. At times Eric would leave his dog with me, and supplied me with a rifle that he taught me how to use. He also brought me food, and some jeans to wear. One night he tried to sneak up on me. He thought he was being funny. Well, I almost shot his head off. He didn't do that again.

I had a friend, Millie whose father used to knock her around. I managed to get a hold of her, and told her what I was doing and asked her if she wanted to run away from home. She did, so I had her join me on the hill. This was much better as now, I wasn't so alone when Eric wasn't there. Eric's mother was beginning to suspect something was going on with Eric. Her groceries were disappearing and she wanted to know where he was spending all his time.

One day Eric brought a friend to our hideout. His name was Dale. The next thing I know we are a foursome. Things take a bad turn. Up until this point in time I had no clue about sex. Eric and I were outside, and Millie and Dale were in the tent. Eric started to paw and kiss me. I didn't mind the kissing, but I didn't like where his hands were trying to go, and I noticed that there was a lump of something in the front of his jeans. He was trying to tell me that he loved me, and that what he was trying to do was a part of it. I didn't understand the love part either. I got pissed off and told him if that was what he wanted, he had better go see Millie! I had heard through the grapevine at school that Millie did things with boys that weren't nice, and I knew that what Eric was trying to do wasn't nice. Well, he did, and Dale came outside. Dale started to kiss and paw on me too. Because I was so pissed at Eric, I let Dale do what he wanted to do. It was disgusting! While we were necking I felt hardness up against me. The next thing I knew, my undies were off, and his pants were on the ground, and he was on top of me, forcing his thing into me. (At the time I didn't know the word for it.) We did it right there on the ground. I didn't like it. When it was over, I noticed blood in between my legs. Later I was told it was because Dale "popped my cherry", whatever that meant. I was now a full-fledged "dumb box of rocks!" Eventually I learned what it meant, the cherry thing.

The time on the hill only lasted for about three weeks. It was autumn and started to get cold, and rainy, and I was getting bored. There were no more episodes of sex. It seemed like everyone had changed. Millie decided to go back home and take her beating for running away. I decided to leave too, except I had no place to go, and very little money. I didn't say anything to Eric, and just up and left. I headed for the city. I roamed around looking for someplace to sleep. I went down to the rail yard, and found a boxcar with the door open. I climbed up in it, and curled up in a corner and went to sleep. I didn't sleep to good because the floor was hard and it was cold, and I was hungry. When I woke up, I knew that I had to do something, I just didn't know what, and then it hit me! I called my social worker! He came and picked me up. He took me to the detention home. This was not the one in the Victorian house. This was a building made of bricks, and there were both boys and girls there. The boys were on one side, and girls on the other.

I liked the detention home. Everyone had their own room. We ate our meals in a large dining room that had several tables. We had no chores, so there was nothing to do except sit around and talk or read. The matron was very nice and taught me how to crochet. The one thing that impressed me the most was that we were all treated the same. Everything was fair. I was there for about two months. The next thing I knew I was going back to my Protestant foster home. The one with the great parents, I was so happy! There was one catch though; it was only for six months, again.

I arrive home and my foster mother and father were happy to see me. I fell back into the family routine, and once again I am happy. I went to church every Sunday, and was doing pretty good in school. I also baby sat to earn money. All the while I kept looking at the calendar. This time I had a plan. I figured it out. One week before it was time for me to leave and go to another foster home, I would run away. This time I had money that I earned from baby-sitting. And this time the adventure got bigger. I also had a new case manager from the Department of Social Services. He was a really nice man and tried talking me into behaving myself. He would even bring me bananas when he came to see how I was doing, because he knew I liked them. He also knew that what had been happening to me in my life wasn't fair, but could do nothing about it. He felt that because I did well in a Protestant foster home, that I should be allowed to stay there, but the rules, were the rules, and he couldn't change them.

I soon discovered that the local bus station was a great hangout, and there were a lot of guys there, especially ones in uniform. I would go there and have a soda or a cup of coffee and soon the guys *would come over and introduce themselves. They always gave me their addresses so that I could write to them, and for the most part I did. I made a lot of acquaintances, and learned that there was an Air Force Base not too far away. Sometimes I would hitch hike to the air base to see one of the guys. I really liked this particular guy, and of course we had sex, and again it was nothing. I couldn't understand what the big deal was about having it, and it always seemed that it was only the guys that wanted to do it. For the most part, I did a lot of hot and heavy necking, and also did a lot of shoving, and saying no. While on a visit I learned about the base hospital, as one of the guys I met was there. We would play cards and talk. After awhile the guys started calling me sunshine. I loved all this attention. But like all good things, this too came to an end, only this time it was the MP's (Military Police). They picked me up coming out of the hospital one day and took me to a room at base headquarters. They didn't do anything to me but warned me not to come on to the base anymore, and then they left me alone in a room. I was waiting for some kind of retribution but it never came, and no one else came to tell me what to do, so I left. It was night, and I didn't leave the base, I went to the PX and drank beer instead. I didn't get caught.*

I had been sleeping in an old car in the local junkyard. In the morning I would get up, walk to the diner across from the base, wash up, and have a cup of coffee, a few smokes, and then go back on the base.

One night I almost froze to death, it was so cold. My sneakers were wet and they became stiff. I thought for sure, my toes were going to freeze and break off. This particular morning I was sitting in the diner when a cop came up and asked me who I was. I gave him a phony name, but it didn't work. The next thing I know I am on my way back to the detention home. Now, I don't know if you have noticed, but I never runaway from home in the summer or spring. It is either late fall, or winter. What was up with that?

I was happy to be back at the detention home. I like the structured way of life. A time to do this, and a time to do that. It is warm, and comfortable and there is good food. I am like a cat with a full tummy, cozy, and content to lie around. I was just waiting to be sent back to my foster home. While waiting to be sent back to my foster home, I met a girl. I don't recall her name, but she didn't like me. One day she and I got into a brawl. It was wild. I got the blame and ended up being locked in my room. I was so pissed! My meals were brought to me, but I wouldn't eat. The black lady that worked in the kitchen felt sorry for me, so at the end of the day she would bring me peanut butter and jelly sandwiches with milk. She was a sweetheart.

I needed to do something because I was so bored. I decided to irritate the hell out of the staff. I managed to use a toothbrush to open the window, so I could talk to the boys next door. I also threw *everything I had around the room. Two staff members, a man and a woman decided that they wanted to take away my shoes for whatever reason. They physically threw me on the bed to do it, and I fought them every inch of the way. They got my shoes, but because I had popped one of them in the midst of the struggle, I was sent to a stripped down room that had only a bed in it. The room wasn't totally ready to be inhabited, as it was still in the process of being finished. I noticed that there wasn't a cover on the switch plate. I still wanted to create havoc so after awhile I took my toothbrush and stuck it into the outlet. This caused the lights to go out in the building, and had the staff scurrying around trying to figure out what had happened. For some insane reason, that I cannot explain, I took a bobby pin and used it to cut up my left arm. When I look back, I thought that it would get me some attention, and it did. After this I got bored again. When one of the staff came to check on me I told him that I was the one that caused the lights to go out. I was hiding my left arm behind my back. He asked to see why. I said no. He came into the room to have a look. When he saw my arm, he freaked. He took me out to a doctor who cleaned and bandaged it up. After that I was taken back to the detention home, but I went back to my previous room without being locked up in solitary confinement. I didn't create anymore trouble after that, and just waited to be sent back to my foster home. The good one. Before long I was taken back there. My foster father was not happy with me and started to raise his voice.*

My foster mother told him to leave me alone, and told him that I had been through enough. Life falls back into a happy rhythm, but I know that my days are numbered, and again I watch the calendar, and again, I runaway when the time for me to leave is at hand.

I went to the city, and somehow met a girl. We became friends. She was tough, and carried a gun. She liked raising hell, and I don't mean the fun kind. One night she and I were out walking the streets, just hanging out. She dared me to pick up a rock and throw it through the window of a dry cleaning store. Not wanting her to think that I was a chicken, I did. We ran. She stopped long enough to bust the windshield of a car with the butt of her gun. I decided that I didn't want that kind of trouble, so I never saw her again. The next day I headed back to farm country.

I decided that I would pop in and see my friend Ann. She lived with her father and older brother. I had no idea where her mother was. Ann let me stay a few days. She was worried that the police would come to her house looking for me. I packed a lunch, and when Ann left for school I hit the highway for another adventure.

I started hitchhiking. Soon, a tractor-trailer stopped and picked me up. I was not afraid, and climb in. The driver was nice. I made up a sob story that I was living with my older sister who was a drunk. I told him that I was sixteen, and he must have believed me because he never said anything. He told me that he was headed for Canada, but would drop me off in a place called Niagara Falls. He had a picture of his wife and kids on his visor. He asked me what I was going to do. I told him that I wanted to get a job. On the way we stopped at a diner, and he bought me a burger and a coke. When we got to Niagara Falls he gave me a dollar so that I could buy a newspaper, and something to eat. He wished me luck, and I never saw him again. I didn't buy a newspaper, because I didn't have a clue about finding a job, and I didn't know a soul.

It was my first day in Niagara Falls, and I was feeling really lonely. I was standing outside a soda shop, when a car full of kids pulled up to the curb. One of the guys got out, walked past me, and went into the store. I noticed that he was checking me out. He came out and got in the car. They sat there for awhile, and then one of the girls yelled over and asked if I wanted to hang out with them. I said yes. What a good time I had. They introduced me to dancing and alcohol. These kids had an old clubhouse left from their younger days. They took me there to spend the night. The next day they dropped me off something to eat on their way to school. The girls got together after school and decided that I should spend the night with one of them at their house.

The girl that I liked was named Lucia. My first two nights were spent at her house, and what a house it was! Lucia had her own room and it was beautiful. Her parents were Italian and there was always something great cooking on the stove, and they liked me. Life was good, and it was heaven. Lucia and I, and two of the guys would go out riding in a car and end up dancing at some bar. We drank, danced, necked and had a good time. The nice thing though... there was no sex. I don't remember ever getting drunk, just buzzing. During the day when Lucia went to school, I would leave too so that her parents would think I was going to school. I would hang around downtown until Lucia got out of school.

There was another girl who wanted me to stay at her house for a few days. I agreed so that the grownups didn't get suspicious. I didn't like this house. It was dirty, drab, and dismal, and there was no human warmth. After one day, I went back to Lucia's house. We gave her parents a sob story about my parents being drunks and beating on me. They said that I could stay for a while longer.

One Saturday, Lucia and I went to the movies to see Marlon Brando in "The Wild Ones". After the movie, we headed to her house. About four houses away from hers we could see a cop talking to her mother. I knew that I couldn't go back to her house and I didn't want her to get into trouble, so I thanked her for all the fun I had, and said goodbye. I still think *about her after all these years, and wonder what became of her.*

After leaving Lucia I was feeling miserable, and the weather was turning cold, and it started to rain. I walked past houses that had lights in the living room windows that gave the appearance of warmth, and kindness. I began to feel alone again, and tired of the hiding. I was walking and wishing that I had a home. I came upon a cop walking the beat. I gave him my name and asked him if he was looking for me. He told me to wait. He went into a store and made a phone call, the next thing I knew I was on my way to another detention home in New York. I liked it there too, but was soon shipped back to my own detention home. It was like "Old Home Day".

The matron said that if I kept coming back that they would have to build a monument in my name. It was good to be back. There was one big problem. I was not going to be sent back to my foster home. Not this time. My case manager couldn't save me, and I know that he felt bad about what was going to happen, but his hands were tied. I had to go before the juvenile judge. He said that he was tired of me running away from home and was going to send me to a Catholic institution run by nuns for wayward girls, whatever they were. I told him that if he sent me there I would probably beat the crap out of the nuns. He then became really upset with me, and sentenced me to do a year in a reform school, whatever that was, and boy, was I going to get a real education in life!

I soon found out that this was not a nice place. It was like a big campus and had a lot of brick houses with Dutch Architecture. They were called cottages. They were anything but that. There was also a school, hospital, beauty parlor, and a little campus store. There was also a baseball diamond. The first place I was sent to was an orientation cottage. This is where they gave you a psychological test, and a physical. The results of your testing would determine which cottage you were sent to. Some cottages had a mother and a father, others didn't.

There were twenty or more girls here. Some were there for running away from home, some were habitual thieves, a few were pregnant, and there was one girl that had killed her boyfriend. I was an angel compared to these girls!

This was my first experience with different ethnic groups, as the girls were made up of Black, Hispanic, and Caucasian. There was even one Jewish girl, and one American Indian. Most of the girls came from down state, and were tough cookies, as I would soon learn. Because there wasn't enough room in my designated cottage, and because they needed my bed in orientation, I was sent to the campus hospital. I stayed there for two days. It was all rather scary, as I didn't know what was going to be happening next. I soon found out, and it wasn't nice.

I was sent to the worst cottage on the campus. It was strict and headed up by a black housemother that had been a sergeant in the United States Army, and she was a bitch. My first night there was quite an experience. I was brought over from the hospital. Everyone in the cottage was up on the second floor where most of the bedrooms were. As I walked up the stairs, I saw a red haired girl with a green face! I thought...what the hell! She disappeared into her room. I was introduced to all the girls and the housemother. I was also told the rules. There were so many of them. I also found out that the girl with the red hair had broken one of the rules, which was, no borrowing. She had borrowed green toothpaste from another girl. The housemother had taken the toothpaste and spread it all over the girl's face to set an example for the others. I felt so bad for that girl with the green face. I was wishing that I could click my heels together and go home, any home, any place but here.

I didn't like this place. I hated it already. I wanted to run. The old timers knew it. When we were out for a walk they would goad me into trying it. They would shove me from behind, and try to get me to run. I wouldn't. I soon found out that if I ran, that would give them an excuse to chase me and beat the shit out of me. I wasn't that stupid! " Dumb as a box of rocks" maybe, but not stupid. In the beginning I had a lot of problems adjusting. I felt like a trapped animal with no way out, and there wasn't.

In my second week, I was in major trouble. There were two black twin sisters, for some reason they decided to cause me a lot of trouble. They went to the housemother and told her that I had been telling them about sex encounters that I had had before I was sent there. They also made up a bunch of other lies. The housemother called all the girls together and held a kind of kangaroo court. The sister's repeated their lies in front of everyone. I was so embarrassed, and humiliated. I denied everything, as I had not even talked to them about my personal life. The next thing I knew I was being sent to my room, and locked in, until I decided to tell the truth. However, there was nothing for me to admit to. I sat on my bed and tried to think of a solution to my dilemma.

I hated this place, and I hated the two sisters for lying. I wanted to be dead. Having no knowledge as to the workings of my digestive system, or where my heart was, I decided to swallow an open safety pin. I thought that the pin would find its way to my heart, stick in, and I would somehow die. Wrong! The damned thing stuck in my throat, and I was scared to the point of hysteria. I pounded on the door until one of the girls came up to see what the racket was all about. I told her what I had done. The next thing you know, up came the housemother and all the girls. This was excitement for them, and as long as everything was focused on me, they weren't getting in trouble. The housemother sent

one of the girls down to the kitchen for a loaf of
bread. The girl came back with a loaf of raisin. The
housemother told her that it was too good for me,
and sent her back down for white bread. Meanwhile,
I kept trying to swallow the pin, but it just kept
sticking in my throat. The girl came back with the
bread. The housemother said I was going to eat the
whole loaf, and I did, in front of everybody. After
the second slice, the pin went down, but I still had
to eat the whole loaf of bread. I thought I was
going to explode, and the humiliation of it all was
more than my mind could handle. The housemother
had two girls remove everything from my room
except my mattress, and they brought me a pot to
use for a toilet, and once again I was locked in. The
housemother said I wasn't going to get out of that
room until I passed the pin, and told the truth. Well,
there was no way I was going to paw through my own
crap to look for it, and I couldn't admit to something
I didn't do, but I had to do something. My brain
was just spinning. I started to formulate a plan. I
needed to get out of that room, and I needed to
become a PC. (Privileged character). Up until this
point I had been watching how things worked in the
line of command.

Downstairs, there were six or seven bedrooms,
along with the kitchen, and dining room. I don't
recall a living room per se. Everything took place
in the dining room, or in the large hallway that led
to the bedrooms on the first floor. These rooms
were occupied by trusted girls that were called PC's

These girls got to do room inspections, and weren't locked in at night. They were also the ones that locked everyone else in, and they were the pets of the housemother.

The daily routine started with your room. Your bed had to be made military style, with hospital corners. You also had to dust everything. Your clothes had to be folded neatly in your drawers. There could be no stains on anything, even on the bottom of your socks. There could be no hair in your hairbrush, not even one strand. Your bedroom floor had to be buffed on your hands, and knees using a piece of an old army blanket. This was the last thing you did on your way out of your room. As soon as you were finished with a broom, dustpan, or polishing rag, you had to return them to the laundry room. You could not make a sound while you were cleaning or walking back and forth in the hallway. The night housemother had an apartment on this floor, and you didn't dare wake her up.

When we were finished doing our room we had to wait for the PC's to come and inspect. If you had one thing wrong, you lost your cigarettes after meals for the day. If you had two things wrong, you lost your cigarette and dessert. If you had three things wrong you lost your cigarette, dessert, and were locked in right after supper.

The set up for the dining room was twisted. There was a long table that faced all the round tables. The housemother, beginners, second and first cooks, sat with her. There was a television on the far wall directly across from the main table. If you were lucky enough to face it, you could watch it while you were eating. If you didn't face it, you couldn't turn around to see what was going on, and you didn't dare try to take a look either.

The meals weren't bad. I had never experienced grits, or side pork before. I didn't mind the grits, but I didn't care for the pork, especially when there was still hair on the rind, but we had to eat it anyway. We had to eat everything. Nothing was wasted. The best part of the meal was the cigarette. We had one after each meal, and one before bedtime.

Before bedtime we would all sit around the housemother in the hallway, either on the floor or on the stairs. We could talk to each other and sometimes we would take turns singing a solo. I always wanted to read, but the housemother wouldn't let me. She said she had no way to know if I was really reading or thinking about something that might get me into trouble. An idle mind is the devil's workshop, and all that, you know.

Meanwhile, back to my isolation. I played the thoughts of what to do, over and over in my head. The only way out of this room was to say that I had lied, and that I did tell those lurid tales to the twins. I didn't want to admit to something that I didn't do, but I didn't want to poke through that pot *either, and I didn't want to stay locked up. After much agonizing I decided to be the world's greatest actress. I would tell them what they wanted to hear. The next day I pounded on the door. One of the PCs came up to see what I wanted. I told her that I wanted to talk to the housemother. A few minutes later she came up with all the girls. I came out and admitted to everything, and even apologized! Inside, I was seething with rage. Those two bitches knew I never told them one damned word, and they sat there looking so smug with smiles on their faces, and I felt that the housemother was aware of it all. She was twisted in her own way. I found that out later.*

On my first day of school I was walking up the stairs to the second floor, when all of a sudden I saw two girls kissing each other! I stopped dead in my tracks. I was shocked, because I was not familiar with this. The next thing I knew I was being shoved from behind and told to move on. And then I heard someone say, "chickie, chickie", and the kissers broke up, and everyone took off to their classrooms. I later found out that chickie was the word used to alert the girls of an oncoming adult. I also learned about lesbianism, and that was why those two girls were kissing. I couldn't imagine the need to kiss another female! However, I did find it all very interesting, and would try to ask questions that no one wanted to answer. The girl who had the room across the hall from me had a girlfriend. Her name was Angel. She looked feminine, but dressed very masculine. She was really a very nice person, and we became friends. It didn't matter to me that she had a kissing girlfriend. I liked her because she was soft spoken and gentle.

To insure that I would never get any demerits for stains in my socks or wrinkled dresses, I would wash them out at night, and wear the same ones every day. This washing was done on a scrub board by hand, with a bar of brown soap. I was determined not to lose my smokes, and I had to move downstairs.

It didn't take me long to become a PC. In one month I was down stairs handling the keys and locking the other girls up. I also became beginners cook. This was no big deal, as all I got to do was wash vegetables, pots, pans, and clean the kitchen floor. It also came about that I would work on the school farm. Because my track record followed me to this hellhole, the powers that be knew I was familiar with farming, so I was picked to help out. I loved it, as it gave me time away from the cottage, and I could work off my anger.

One day at mail call I received a check for sixty dollars. I couldn't believe it, and thought there must have been a mistake. Come to find out, it was a Social Security check, from my father's death. I couldn't keep it, but could draw on it to buy things at the campus store. The funny thing about everyone shopping was that we all would buy crap to give to the housemother. We would go to the store, and when we got back to the cottage, the housemother would be sitting in this chair at the top of the stairs like she was some kind of royalty. We would gather around her and give her the stuff. I can remember myself thinking two things. One, who in hell did she think she was, for sitting there waiting for us to bestow our goodies on her, and two, this was a bribe, and we who were lucky enough to have money, could insure ourselves of an easier life. This sucked, but was a necessary evil.

Because my behavior record was so good, I got to take the train home for Christmas. I went back to the nice foster home for a week, but something had changed. I didn't feel the same about anything, not even my beloved Christmas. Maybe it was boring, maybe it was because I didn't belong, but things felt different. I can't explain it. It didn't even bother me to go back to the school when the holidays were over.

When I returned to the hellhole I met a woman who visited the reform school. She took an interest in me. She asked to have me go to her house once a week to help her clean. I never did clean, but we would just have lunch and talk. One day she took me shopping with her. She knew I loved to read, so she told me to pick out a book, and she would buy it for me. I did. It was "Battle Cry", a World War II story. The only thing I knew was that I couldn't be caught with it, because I wasn't supposed to be reading. I managed to sneak it into the cottage, and

I would read it after lights out. There was a light outside my bedroom window, and I would use this to read by. I would also hide the book in the cellar and read it when I was working in the kitchen. I always found an excuse to go down, so I could read a page, or two. Whenever I had the chance to read it I would. I loved war stories, and this one had romance and humor, so it was really good.

One day one of the girls that worked in the kitchen wanted to run away. She wanted me to help her, but I didn't want anything to do with it, I wasn't that stupid. Because I wouldn't take part in her scheme, she blew me in about the book. I didn't even know that she knew. The housemother raged at me, and I denied having it. She sent one of the girls down to look for it, and as I waited I was shitting myself. I had hidden it so well that no one could find it. Was I ever lucky! I never read another book in that cottage again.

The housemother had a brutal streak. She liked to make some of the girl's cry, and at times some of us were a part of her brutality in one way or another. There are a few instances that really stick in my memory. There was the time when a young black girl was degraded in front of the rest of us for not taking a shower. Housemother said she stunk. She ordered me and two other girls to take her into the shower, strip her, and scrub her down with a real scrub brush. None of us really wanted to do this, but we had no choice. We were PC's. We took the girl into the shower room and let her take her own clothes off. We had a plan. The girl would get in the shower, and take it, and while she was washing we would have her scream as if we were really scrubbing her, and we would be yelling like we meant it. It worked. Housemother was happy. At another time, a new girl came to our cottage. She was tall and blonde, and she walked with her back very straight and her head up. Kind of like a snob. No one liked her, and she hated the reform school worse than I did. I didn't have to talk to her to know this. One day there were visitors from the state. They would come periodically to check out the school to make sure that it was being run efficiently and in the proper manner. The blonde girl was watching from her bedroom window and saw them outside. She proceeded to put her fists through the glass and was screaming and yelling that she wanted to get out and go home. I grabbed the keys and went running to her room. I opened the door, and there was blood all over her arms. The housemother came upstairs to have a look. She was pissed! She made the girl go down to the bathroom/ laundry room to wash the blood off. The housemother followed her in. The door was open and you could hear the housemother yelling at the girl. The next thing I knew the girl came flying out the door, hit the wall, and collapsed in a heap on the floor. Housemother had grabbed her bodily and threw her across the room and out the door. I thought the girl was dead. It was scary. Those of us that witnessed this were dismissed to go about our business. The next day the blonde girl was gone. I found out, that if you were to act crazy, they sent you to a hospital, and then you went home, it only happened once during my stay there.

The last incident made me formulate an escape from this cottage. There was a little fat Jewish girl that was sent to our place. She was very quiet, and very frightened. Kind of like a fat, gentle little rabbit. The housemother didn't like her. One morning the girl made too much noise walking down the hall. The housemother made her walk on her tiptoes for about an hour as a form of punishment. I don't remember what happened next, but the girl dripped blood on the floor from somewhere on her body. Housemother was really pissed! She made the girl strip all the wax from the hardwood hallway floor, and then made her wax it again. This was done on your hands and knees. It wasn't liquid wax, but paraffin, and you would put it on in the same way you would write with chalk, except you made lines with it across the boards. You would use an old army blanket to buff the wax out and bring it to a shine. This was harder than hell, and seemed to take forever. I felt so bad for this girl, but could not interfere. I did not want to experience housemother's wrath, and I wanted out of this nightmare. I decided to get sick, but in the beginning it was legitimate.

It all started with a cough. No one could figure out why I had it, so they sent me to the campus hospital. I had a small fever, so they kept me there. They put a vaporizer in my room, but gave me no real medicine. I loved it. As soon as I noticed that my fever had disappeared, I came up with an idea that would keep me there until my time at the school was up. Three times a day a nurse would come in and take my temperature. She would put the thermometer in my mouth and then leave. While she was gone, I would take the thermometer, and hold it in front of the steam. I would then shake it down to around 100, or 101. This constant temperature had them puzzled, so they took me into the local town for chest x-rays. There was nothing there, but they continued to keep me in the hospital because of my cough, (which I faked, and my contrived fever). Now, I was happier than pigs in shit! The food was great, and you didn't have to do any kind of chores. There were two or three other girls there too, and we were able to socialize without fear of being reprimanded. The only thing we couldn't do was visit with each other in our rooms. At first I didn't understand why, but then I figured it out. It was the lesbian thing. However, all I thought that being a lesbian was about, was just kissing. For years I had no clue about what lesbians really did.

The head nurse had been a Lieutenant in the Army, and she was exceptionally nice to me. Sometimes she even spent time with me, and I told her about what was going on at the cottage. The only thing she had to say about it was that many years before I had come there, it was far worse. From our conversations she found out that I liked to draw pictures, so she went out and bought me art supplies, and had me draw her some pictures, and I could read to my heart's content. I was in heaven! But just outside of heaven, hell loomed, and the fear of being sent back to that cottage was with me constantly.

One day I was walking past one of the girls rooms. She was in bed. She called for me to come in. The coast was clear, so I did. This girl was black, and I liked her. I was standing by her bed when she reached up, pulled my head down, and kissed me. I was flabbergasted! A girl, kissing me! I felt nothing, and I don't think she did either because it never happened again. It was all so very weird.

I stayed in the hospital for two months, and then was released one month before my sentence was up. There was a buzz going around that I had gotten the housemother into a lot of trouble. Before my release I was accompanied by someone and went back to the cottage to get my things. The only thing I remember about my leaving was that housemother said that I would be back and she was glaring at me. She said everyone comes back. I told her that she would never see me again, and she didn't. I would live in fear until I either got married, or turned eighteen, but I never went back. I think I was fifteen years old.

My new home was with a nice Italian Family. They had several children. All were grown and married except one, and she was going to nursing school.

There were two other foster girls there. They had never been to reform school, but had their own problems. This home wasn't bad, and they really did try to make us feel that we were a part of their family. We had a curfew. On school nights we had to be in by ten o'clock, and on Friday's and Saturday's we got to stay out until eleven. However, I still felt as if I didn't belong, but I would make the best of it because in no way did I want to get sent back to reform school.

On my first day of school I ran into my friend Ann from my farm days. She was a Lieutenant in the Civil Air Patrol and asked me to join. This was a big deal, as my goal was to join the Air Force as soon as I graduated from high school. This was the auxiliary of The United States Air Force! Once again I was happy, and everything seemed to be going in the right direction, but as usual the fickle finger of fate was pushing me in other directions.

I went to school every day, and became popular with my classmates. This popularity didn't last long. I managed to go through a year and a half of school in three months. The reason I was able to do this was because I wanted to quit and get a job. I talked with a guidance counselor about my reasons for quitting. One of the reasons was because I was the oldest kid in my class. She said that if I could prove to her that I could do the work, she would move me ahead. I did, but some of the kids were jealous. I became a sophomore. The time had come for the sophomore dance and they were looking for a King and a Queen. I was voted to be Queen. I was thrilled because now I really felt like somebody. I went and picked out my gown and fantasized about the dance, and how it would be. Well, it wasn't to be. Something happened. I went to go to a meeting about the dance, and a girl told me that I wasn't really the queen and it had all been a mistake. I was blown away! I couldn't believe it! I never went back to that school again. I transferred to one closer to my house. I never even knew if that girl was telling the truth, but I didn't hang around to find out. I was so humiliated.

During the summer I liked to go to the amusement park on the lake. Sometimes one of my foster sister's and I would go. She had a boyfriend that had a car, and he would take us. This one particular day she brought along her brother. He was about my age. We spent most of the day necking, just necking, without doing any thing else. This was boring, and the only thing I got from all that necking was a sore on my chin that soon turned into something called impetigo. We took her brother home and went back to the park. We just hung out, laughed and had a good time. One problem, it was getting later, and later. Soon, it was dark, and we were past our curfew. We were in deep shit! We had her boyfriend drop us off about two blocks away from the house. We tried to concoct a story that would explain our being so late getting home. I don't remember what the story was, but I do remember that the only thing *that happened was that we were both grounded that weekend. No reform school!*

I went to school, and worked part time in a hospital. I would deliver food trays to patients and wash glasses. I emptied wastebaskets and fluffed pillows. I liked it, and everyone liked me, and best of all, I earned my own money. One day I was working in the maternity ward. Now, it wasn't my job to handle bedpans, but there was one woman who had been sitting on one for quite awhile. She asked me to take it. I told her that it wasn't my job. She was such a bitch! She started screaming and yelling at me to do it, and I did, not because I wanted to or had to, but subconsciously, I must have felt that if I didn't, I would end up back in reform school. I look back at it now, and realize how stupid I was, but that was my mindset at the time.

I began to notice that guys were starting to look at me, and found me to be pretty. I liked this feeling, and I started to flirt. There was an older man that was my neighbor. His name was Tony. He was good looking and I noticed him checking me out. One day I was on my way to a Civil Air Patrol meeting. I was waiting for the bus. He pulled up in his car and asked me if I wanted a ride. I said no, because I couldn't get a wrinkle in my uniform, and I had to ride the bus standing up. I was all excited that this guy wanted to be with me. At some point in time we did get together. We went and parked up at Lover's Hill. Hell! I didn't even know what a lover was at that point in my life, but I would soon learn. This guy and I were in the back seat of his car. We were kissing, and we were going at it hot and heavy, and it was beginning to feel good. He had just started to take his pants down, when all of a sudden there was a flashlight shining on us. It was a cop and Tony got a ticket. I didn't know what the ticket was for and I freaked. I thought for sure that I was going to be sent back to reform school. Tony knew a cop on the force and got a hold of him to take care of the ticket. He did. Tony and I were never alone together after that. I wanted to, but didn't realize that I was something referred to as jailbait. I chased him with a vengeance. I wanted to kiss and be touched the way we had done that night on the hill. He finally explained what would happen if we were caught. He would go to jail, and I would definitely end up back at reform school. I don't think I cared if he went to jail, but I did care about where I would end up. However, I always lived on the edge. The thought of reform school was always in the back of my head, but it didn't seem to really stop me from doing what I wanted to do. Go figure. It must have been living with the thrill of getting caught or getting away with the dirty deed, or I was as "dumb as a box of rocks." I never did figure it out.

As time went on, I met a nice Jewish Boy. He was going to the local college and studying to become a lawyer. In the summer he worked at a resort, and would bring me little gifts when he came home. One night we ended up on the couch in a friend's house.

We were necking hot and heavy, and it was just like that time with Tony, and the next thing I knew, he was on top of me and his thing was inside of me. It didn't feel good. I didn't like his thing in me, but I liked the hugging and kissing part, so we did it every time we had a chance. Why I never got pregnant, I will never know. Of course, I didn't even know about pregnancy being and end result of what I was doing. Whenever I would get home after a date with him, my foster mother would tell me that he would never marry me because he was a Jew, and I was a Gentile. I didn't even know what a Gentile was, or a Jew for that matter. After awhile I saw this guy less, and less. Before long, I wasn't seeing him at all. I didn't even feel bad.

Being in the Civil Air Patrol was fun. We had flight parties, and I got to meet guys. I met a photographer who wanted me to be a model for him. He said that I would eventually model for appliances and clothing. I was flying high, and happy once again. He took a lot of different poses of me. Some were in sweaters, costumes, and a lot of bikini shots. I thought I was hot stuff, and in a sense, I was. I had a feeling of power, but never figured out what it was. Not until I was much older, and it was too late, did I realize that it was sex. That word wasn't even a part of my vocabulary back then.

While in the Civil Air Patrol I met a guy that I fell in love with. He was in The United States Air Force. His name was Phillip. He was both handsome and rich. I met him at a flight party, and we started to go steady. He gave me a ring. Sometimes we would go to my girlfriend Ann's house and hang out or we would go to the movies. We started talking about getting married. When we were at my girlfriend's house we did a lot of heavy necking and petting, but he never tried to put his thing in me. He touched me all over and he put a fire inside of me. I wanted his thing in me, but he wouldn't do it. He used his hands and made me feel wonderful. Come to find out, that wonderful feeling was called a climax, and I loved it. Whenever we were alone he would give me what I wanted. He never went all the way with me because he thought I was a virgin, and I didn't let him know otherwise. By now I had found out what a virgin was, and I also knew that I wasn't one.

It was a known fact among our friends that we were going to be married. One night Phillip had something called CQ Duty at his barracks and couldn't go to a flight party. I went without him. There was a guy there who was dating one of my girlfriends. She wasn't there either. The two of us just talked. He asked me if I would go to dinner with him. I said yes. I didn't see a problem with this, as it was on the up and up, with no hanky panky. Well, his girlfriend got so pissed off when she found out, that she went to Phillip and told him that I wasn't a virgin. She didn't even know whether I was, or wasn't. No one knew except me. The next thing I knew, Phillip was always busy. One day I was downtown shopping and I ran into Eric. He was just out of The Army. He asked me for my phone number and I gave it to him. This business with Phillip pissed me off, and I didn't care, so the next time Phillip called, I told him about Eric. I also told him that because we hadn't been seeing each other I was going to date Eric. In a sarcastic voice he said," I hope the two of you will be very happy for the rest of your life", and little did I know what my twisted future had in store for me, and I am now seventeen.

Phillip stopped by my house one Saturday to give me an invitation to his graduation, from the university. He had been taking The Russian language for his Air Force assignment. When he gave me the invitation, I gave him back his ring, and everything was called off. There would be no wedding. I wasn't even sure I wanted to go to his graduation, but I did. After the ceremony I waited around for him. He didn't show up. A friend of his came up to me and offered to look for him. He thought that he might have been saying goodbye to his professors. He went back in to look for him. No dice, he wasn't there. His friend had a car and we went over to the barracks to look for him. We pulled up. Phillip came out all happy with a bottle of champagne in one hand, and his orders in the other. He looked so damned cute! He came over to the car and kissed me, as if nothing had happened. He said that he was being sent to Japan, but that he had a thirty-day leave before he shipped out. He was going to go back home, which was out of state. He said that he would call me later when he got home. That was the last I saw of him. His friend drove me home. I went right up to my room and cried all day. I knew in my heart, that I really loved Phillip, and I thought he really loved me. It wasn't until later that he would declare his love for me, but then...it would be too late. My foster mother kept trying to get me to come out and eat, but I wanted nothing except Phillip. I played songs that reminded me of him, and I just kept crying, until there were no more tears left inside me. Later that evening my older brother Bill happened to stop by. My foster mother came up to my room and begged me to go for a ride with him. She said that it would make me feel better. It had been awhile since I had seen him, so I gave in and went. What a mistake that was! When I returned home, I found out that Phillip had called just after I left, and he never called again. The fickle finger of fate was indeed twisted, and wreaking havoc with my life.

Eric called me all the time. He was relentless. He had a motorcycle, and we would go on long rides. By now I had quit school in my junior year, and was working a full time job. He kept hounding me to marry him, and I kept saying no. I was only seventeen, and I wanted to go into The Air Force, but couldn't join until I was eighteen. Back then I don't believe that you had to be a high school graduate. The one thing I was sure of was that in no way did I want to get married now, or ever. From the time Phillip left, which was in early May, until the middle of June, my life was fast paced, and hectic.

My job was that of a salesperson, and I didn't mind it as I got to meet people. Our registers had broken down one day, and they sent in a repairman to work on them. At the end of the day, he asked me if I wanted to go for a drink after work. I said yes, and away we went. The place was dimly lit and I easily passed for eighteen. We didn't stay long and he brought me home. He had just pulled away from the curb when Eric roared up on his motorcycle. My foster mother came to the door and urged me to get in the house. Eric got off his motorcycle and threw it on the ground. He started yelling at me and asking questions about where I had been and what I was doing. He grabbed my arm while he was yelling. The next thing I knew, he let go of me, hopped on his motorcycle and tried to catch the repair man. I went in the house and he came back to apologize. He said he caught the repairman and questioned him, and realized that he had made a mistake in accusing me of wrongdoing. I don't think he ever really caught up with him. He just wanted to appear big and bad.

I continued to date Eric because he was rather exciting with his motorcycle, and he was good looking. Where were my brains, on vacation? Or was I just "dumb as a box of rocks?" I went over to Eric's house for dinner one Sunday. After dinner his mother left us alone, and again he asked me to marry him, and again I said no. I told him that I didn't want to get married, and that I wanted to go into The Air Force. He raised his voice, and told me to go on into my damned Air Force. I was upset with his attitude and walked into the foyer and sat down to gather my thoughts. My decision was still the same. No getting married. I went into the living room. He was sitting with his head in his hands. When he looked up, I saw tears streaming down his face, and I blurted out the words that would change my life forever. "Okay! I'll marry you"! He was thrilled to death, and I was in a state of shock! I told him that I didn't love him the way a wife should love her husband, and he told me that I would learn to love him. Can you believe that? And I swallowed it hook, line, and sinker! This was going to be one adventure that I would never forget, and it had stupid written all over it, and I wasn't even eighteen yet, and obviously didn't know the meaning of the word stupid! All the bells, and alarms were going off while the red flag waved! I didn't hear a thing. I was dumbstruck!

Eric's mother signed for him to get married because he was only nineteen. We forged a baptismal certificate that made me look like I was eighteen, because I was only seventeen, and off we went to the town hall for the wedding license accompanied by his mother.

My foster mother didn't have a clue as to what was going on, and I knew she didn't like Eric, so I never told her that we were going to be married, I just left home one day without a word of goodbye. Eric and I, and one of his buddies took off on our motorcycles to go to a big bike rally that was out of state. We found a Baptist Minister to marry

us before we went over the state line. His buddy
was our best man. The Minister looked like he was
scared to death of us. He kept pulling at his groin
area while he was talking. My wedding ensemble
consisted of a pair of Levi jeans with a patch in the
right leg, black engineer boots, and a leather jacket.
I had never dreamed in my wildest dreams that I
would ever be married in such a fashion.

There was nothing exciting or wonderful about
being married, except that I was a runaway, afraid
of being caught and sent back to reform school. We
made it to the rally, and got a hotel room, and then
went out to look around and see what was going on.
This part was a lot of fun, as I had never seen so
many motorcycles in one place, and so many weird,
looking people. It was like Halloween, and then we
went back to our room. Of course he wanted to put
his thing inside me, and he kissed me and touched
me. I didn't like it at all. I didn't even like his touch
at the time. I ended up sleeping with my clothes on.
I have no idea why I did that, but I think it was like
a warning device. If he tried to unbutton my jeans,
I would wake up, and stop him from pawing me.

The rally was one good time, and it was the first
time I had ever seen a motorcycle race. It would be
one of many. Eric didn't try to touch me again until
we got back home.

We moved in with Eric's mother and stepfather until
we could get a place of our own. We had a wedding

reception down in the basement, of his mother's house, and I just knew the tongues were wagging in whispers, about why we ran off and got married. They were wrong.

One evening Eric's friend stopped by, and they were sitting in the kitchen talking with Eric's mother. I was upstairs but could hear their conversation, and it wasn't nice. Eric's mother was telling Eric's friend how Eric could have done better for himself, and how Eric had married beneath him. I couldn't believe my ears! I hated all of them! I went into the bedroom, and took Eric's rifle. I really think that I was going to kill them, but before I could get down the stairs with the rifle, Eric came up and caught me. He asked me what I was doing with it, and I told him. He grabbed it from me and put it away, and he was angry. He went back down stairs and told everyone what I had almost done. His friend said, "that a woman with a knife was one thing, but a woman with a gun was worse," so he got up and left. I went to bed, and left Eric and his mother alone. I really hated all of them, and I hated living in that house.

Eric and I managed to find work together pitching tents for fireman's field days. We traveled around the state doing this, and it was kind of fun, except sometimes we had to sleep in the car. We were what was referred to now as "carnies", and the two of us could put up tents faster than some of the larger crews. This job only lasted through the summer, and early autumn. When it was over, it was back to his mother's house to live.

Eric found a mobile home in a trailer park. We moved in. I found another job right away. It was across from the park, so I didn't have too far to walk. Our so-called love life was a bitch. I would lock myself in the bathroom just before bedtime, and wait for Eric to fall asleep before I climbed into bed, and I slept in my jeans and shirt. That way if he tried anything in the night I would know. This in it's self was stupid, because he just took no for an answer only so many times, and then I would have to give in anyway. Sex was no fun.

One night Eric showed up at my job to have me sign a check. I asked him what is was for, and he just kept insisting that I sign it. It was for five hundred dollars and it was mine! And my head was swimming with the thought that I had so much money. I kept pushing to find out where it came from, and he kept pushing me to sign it, and he was getting pissed. Finally he told me that it was from The Social Security Administration. It was the last check that I would get from them, as I had by now, turned eighteen years old. I had to get back to my job, so I signed it. I had no clue what he did with the money, and I didn't dare ask.

About 6 months after I was married, my foster mother called to tell me that I had a letter from Phillip. (I had since called her and told her what had *happened to me.) I couldn't believe it! My stomach was in knots! I had to get that letter without Eric knowing what I was going home for. I made up a lie telling him that my foster mother found some old photos from my modeling days, and that I wanted to go and pick them up. I told him that I would take the bus, but he insisted on giving me a ride. When I got to her house, she was waiting for me on the porch. She handed me the letter, and my heart was pounding so hard I thought it would jump out of my chest! I didn't know what to do. I wanted to read it right there, but I didn't want Eric to see me doing it. I put the letter in my pocket. I got in the car. Eric asked me where the pictures were. I told him that they were in my pocket. He wanted to see them right then and there. I had no choice but to tell him the truth. He got pissed off and wanted the letter. I wouldn't give it to him. My foster mother was on the porch watching us, and he knew it. I opened the letter, and he made me read it out loud. It was the greatest news in the world, but it was too late. Phillip apologized for being such a fool, and told me that he still loved me and wanted me to be his wife. He would send me the money to meet him in Japan, and we would be married there. My mind went crazy, and was whirling around. All I could think of was why? I wanted to be with him more than anything else in the world, and I was crushed by my own stupidity. I didn't even have the opportunity to mentally record the address. Eric grabbed the letter and tore it up. I never even had a chance to send an answer back to him. He never knew that I* still loved him, and that my marriage to Eric was a big mistake. I know in my heart that if I could have mentally recorded his address that I would have written to him and told him what had happened. He would have forgiven me, and I would have divorced Eric. Phillip, and I could have picked up where we had left off. And I do believe that my life with him would have been almost perfect. Obviously fate had another idea, and I was stuck with the miserable decision I had made. Emotionally, I was devastated, and Eric was super pissed. He was yelling something at me about being his wife. How horrible it all was.

Eric didn't have a job, but he was always working on cars. My pay went to him automatically. He put his hand out on payday, and I gave him my money. It was so automatic for me. I must have resented it, but don't remember how I felt about it at the time. I lost my job as a sales person, but got another one right away. Again, it was across the street, and I would come home for lunch. One day I came home for lunch to find a strange woman in the trailer. He introduced her to me. Her name was Julie. It seems that she was a friend of a friend who wanted to get back with her husband, and we were going to take her to Vermont after I got out of work. Funny thing, when I got home the door was locked and I had to pound on it to get in. Eric finally answered the door, and told me he had to lock it because the dog was jumping up against it, making it pop open. And...I believed him. When would I ever learn?

On the way to Vermont I got sleepy. I was tired from work, and it was a long ride. It was suggested that Julie could sit up front with Eric, and I could catch some sleep in the back seat. I agreed, like a dummy. Every now and then my eyes would open and I would notice how close Julie was sitting to Eric, still not knowing what was going on, I fell back to sleep. I heard the car doors being shut but I didn't think anything of it, and it seemed to come from far away. It seemed that the two of them decided to let me sleep while they got coffee and something to eat. I never even knew the car had stopped. I knew nothing until they got back in. I was beginning to feel that something was wrong but I didn't know what it is. We arrived at this little house where Julie had lived with her parents. They were very poor and the house had only the bare minimum in furniture. There was no place for me to sit down, so I went and attempted to sit on Eric's knee. I say attempted, because he pushed me away twice. Now, I am really getting some kind of message, but I just can't read it. We finally left for home. Going back was very quiet, as neither of us talked, and all the time, I am trying to figure out the message. We got back home and I went to work. When I returned for my lunch, Eric wasn't talking. I went back to work. When I came home, I decided to ask him what was the matter. His answer was that he was in love with Julie! I was stunned at first. I don't remember what I had said, but he went back to the bedroom, and left me there to chew on what he just told me. I went nuts! I grabbed the newspaper and was tearing it up and throwing it around. I was also crying. I was crying over the betrayal, and I cried for Phillip, and I cried over my miserable life. I couldn't understand why he did this to me, so I just up and left.

I remembered a girl that I knew who had an apartment. I went there. She was now married, but let me stay with her for a while. I didn't work, but would go downtown and hang out at a diner that I used to visit when I went to school. The owner was old enough to be my father, and he would let me peel onions and cut up peppers for something to do. There were always a bunch of guys hanging out there, and one of them was divorced with a little girl. I didn't even know what divorce was yet, except that I knew he wasn't with his wife.

I liked the little girl, and her father was handsome. He was friendly as were the other men, but that was it. I never realized that he was getting ideas about me. One day I was walking down town when this guy came along in his car. He had a friend with him that I had never seen before. He yelled out to me and asked me if I wanted a ride. Because I knew him, and trusted him, I said yes. Not even thinking, I got in and sat between the two of them. The next thing I know we were out in the boondocks. The guy that I knew pulled out a knife and put it to my throat. He ordered me to get in the back seat. I did. He told me that if I made one sound that he would cut up my pretty face so that no one would ever look at me again, and then he raped me. When he was finished, his friend raped me. (At the time I didn't know that forced sex was called rape.) I didn't find this out until many years later either. They left me there to walk back to the city. I don't even remember how I felt. I must have been in a state of shock. I couldn't believe that this guy did this to me. I thought he was my friend. I never went back to the diner again, and I never told anyone because I was embarrassed. Besides, back then people didn't report that sort of thing. For years I fantasized how I could kill the bastard. I would visualize myself hiding in some bushes with a rifle that had a silencer on it and killing him. No one would ever know who did it. I lived this dream for years and years, and finally it went away.

Eventually I got another job, and found a room in an apartment house. I wasn't happy and was always afraid that someone would break in. I also answered an ad in the newspaper for a modeling job. It was for modeling in the nude, and the money was good. I don't remember how much I made but it must have been enough, or I would have never done it. After the sessions, the photographer chased me around the studio. He wanted sex, but I wasn't going to let him have it, so I got the hell out of there and never went back. I couldn't understand why in hell every man wanted to have sex. It made no sense to me. As far as I was concerned it was a waste of time.

Before long Eric found me and asked me to go back home with him. I did. It was better than living in fear. Life was a little better and I became pregnant. Now, how did that happen? Eric got a job. We moved out of the trailer park and stayed with his mother for a while. Eric found another trailer that he remodeled. We moved outside the city, and into the country. We had no toilet in our trailer, and it was very small, but compact. The park had public bathrooms with showers that we were able to use. It also had clothes washing facilities. The only problem with that was the water was so hard that when I dried my husband's blue jeans they could stand by themselves. Life was pretty good. I still didn't like sex, and tried to avoid it as much as possible. We had no T.V, just a radio. While Eric was at work I would embroider little clothes for my upcoming baby. My mother-in-law became concerned about my being left alone in my condition while Eric was at work. She decided that we would move in with her and her family. This was not good, as I knew that Eric's mother didn't really like me. I overheard her on the phone one day telling someone again, that Eric could have done better. We moved in. Eric's little sister was a spoiled bitch. She got whatever she wanted, and was a source of irritation for me, as I didn't like her. One day she irritated me so bad that I smacked her in the face. When her mother came home she told her what I had done. She threatened me with everything but the kitchen sink. I let her have it back, and I knew she was afraid of me, but

I never hit the little bitch again, and she left me alone.

On January 5th, in 1959, my water broke. It was a slow leak, and not a gush. My pains were nothing in the beginning and were coming two minutes apart. My mother-in-law became nervous and insisted that I go to the hospital. Eric took me. He couldn't stay with me, because back then it wasn't allowed. It would be the longest two days of both our lives. I thought I knew physical pain. I was wrong. I had been in hard labor for two days, and the birth was dry, and no pain could compare to this. (Except kidney stones) The doctor decided to use forceps to pull the baby out. I had to be cut, to help the baby be born. It was a boy and his head was so pointed that he looked like a comic character called Denny Dimwit. My mother-in-law was upset when she saw him. She thought his head would stay like that. The nurses assured her that it wouldn't. I was happy to have it over with, and excited that I had a baby boy. Eric was happy too. We called him Thomas, Tommy for short.

We stayed with Eric's family for a while, and then when Tommy was six months old we moved to Mesa Arizona. Eric had built a trailer to put our furniture and stuff in. We packed up our belongings, the dog, and the baby, and away we went. This was going to be one hell of an adventure. Half of the back seat was partitioned off for the dog, and the baby had the other half. We had a flat tire in Columbus

Ohio, but that was it, until we hit New Mexico, and then we broke down again. I found the Southwest to have an unusual beauty with wide-open spaces, but it was too damned hot. Some of the roads we had to use were nothing more than mule paths and heaven help you if you were on the side of a mountain with oncoming traffic. However, back then there was hardly any traffic anywhere in the Southwest so we didn't come upon that problem. Going through the desert, I saw a huge snake on the side of a rock near the road. I had never seen anything like it, even in the movies. It was scary. We pushed on to Mesa. The baby was good all the way across the country, and never complained.

We arrived in Mesa and looked for a place to stay. We found a motel with efficiency units and a swimming pool. We set up housekeeping. In two days Eric found a job working on tractor-trailers. The people that stayed there were very friendly. They warned me to shake out my boots and check the beds before climbing in, because of the spiders, snakes, and lizards. While Eric worked, I spent the day in the pool. Sometimes I would bring Tommy in with me, and when I didn't there was an older lady that offered to watch him while I swam and kept cool. Her apartment was air-conditioned. Our unit wasn't. After about a month I wanted to try horseback riding. I loved it! Every morning I would get up and go riding from five am to seven, and then I would go riding from seven to nine at night. Eric was home at these times, so I was able to go.

After two months of living in the motel we found a small house for rent that was just about next door to the motel, and we rented it. Life was good, or so I thought. Little did I know what was going on while I was off horseback riding. Eric was acting strange towards me again. You would think that by now I would recognize the signs. One evening he told me that he was in love with a girl called, Blondie. She lived next door to the motel with her mother. I was shocked! How could this be! I told him that I was going to leave him and I did. I found a job at a riding stable with a room off the office, and I moved in. I kept Tommy with me all day and night. He spent the majority of time in his playpen. He was a good baby. While he played I worked. There was another wrangler that worked there also, and we would take turns roping and saddling up horses for the customers so that I would have time with Tommy. Even when I was in the corral I could see him through the doorway. The only thing I didn't like was the nights. It was scary.

Next door to the stables was a tavern, and I could hear the drunks, laughing and raising hell. I slept with my clothes on, and kept a small handgun under my pillow. I also had a hunting knife that I kept handy, just in case. And don't think I wouldn't have used them if the need had presented it's self. I really liked the job, but I didn't like the fear, so I decided to go home and see if Eric had changed the way he felt about me. I left Tommy with the older couple and went home. Eric wasn't there, so I hung out and waited. When I heard him coming I thought I would be cute, and hid behind the bedroom door. When he came in, I jumped out and yelled boo. He didn't smile. I asked him why he fell in love with Blondie. He told me to look at myself in the mirror. I did, but didn't see anything wrong with how I looked, so I asked him what he meant. He told me that I looked like a man. I always wore jeans, shirts, and boots. I was pissed! I told him that I had never dressed like this before I met him, which was true. The only time I wore jeans was on Saturday when I cleaned house and that was it. I never wore them in public. He said that Blondie was so feminine and pretty and that she always dressed up. I had to remind him that was because she was a secretary in a hospital, and that she had no choice. I couldn't wear dresses, because I worked with horses. After a time of talking it was decided that I would move back home because of Tommy. Life returned to normal once again.

I had an opportunity to sing Country Music on the local radio station. I went for an audition, and was accepted. The people loved me, and I had even received fan mail. I was flying high! And just as fast as I flew up, my husband shot me right back down. One night after the show I was practicing with a band when he came to pick me up. When he saw me with all those guys, he was livid, and told me that I couldn't sing anymore, and he didn't let me. I knew I was good and could have made it in the music *business, but the dream was squashed by the man that was supposed to love, and want the best for me. Yeah...right.*

We found another small house and moved. An older couple that were our friends rented the house in front of ours, so we were somewhat together like a family. This house was really adorable, and I was happy, and then...Eric lost his mind. He really lost his mind.

I have to tell you this, I think that happiness is a condition of the mind, when the mind is out of condition, and how much of a mind could I have when I was as "dumb as a box of rocks?"

Eric suffered from sinus problems, and had headaches. He had been complaining about them because they weren't going away. I didn't realize how bad they were getting until one morning when I had to run after him. He had gotten out of bed and disappeared. I went outside just in time to see him walking down the street in his underwear! I couldn't imagine what was going on. I took his hand and brought him back in to the house. I also caught him loading and unloading his pistol. I had to take the shells and hide them. I had to watch his every movement for fear he would do something stupid, or hurt himself. I knew that something was wrong, but didn't know what. This went on for two weeks. He couldn't work and we had no money. I had to steal bread from our friends when they weren't home, so that I could make peanut butter and jelly sandwiches for us to eat. I didn't ask them for the bread because for some reason I was ashamed to.

I went to our friends and asked the woman what she thought. She suggested that I take him to a doctor. She helped me find one, and I took him on the bus. The doctor wanted to put Eric in the hospital, but we didn't have health insurance, and we had not been in Mesa long enough to be eligible for help. The doctor said that the reason he didn't know who he was, or what he was doing, was because the sinuses had filled, and couldn't drain. They were putting pressure on his brain. The doctor managed to fix the problem temporarily, but said that Eric needed surgery or this problem would reoccur. We decided to sell everything and move back East, and I was pregnant again, and how did that happen?

We took the train back and of course, I loved it. In Kansas City, Eric had gotten off the train for some reason. The train started to pull out of the station and he wasn't back in his seat. I was scared shitless! I left Tommy in the care of a stranger and went running towards the back of the train. I went through several cars but couldn't find him. My head was spinning as I went back to my seat. I didn't know what I was going to do. I thought he was in Kansas City and I was on my way back to New York without him. I got back to my seat, and there he was! As if nothing had happened! I was mad, and he thought it was funny. It seemed that he had gone to the men's room when he got back on the train, and dummy that I was, didn't even think of that.

When we arrived home, Eric's mother met us at the train station. We moved in with her for a while until we could get our own place. She was not happy to hear that I was pregnant and suggested that I get an abortion. Right off the bat the rumor started that the baby wasn't Eric 's. I didn't even know what an abortion was, and had to have her explain it to me. I couldn't believe that she would even suggest such a thing. When I would take a bath, I would pat and rub my growing stomach and cry. To think... she wanted me to kill my unborn baby. It made me so sad and miserable. Eric found an apartment upstairs over a grocery store. It wasn't a bad place, and we settled in. Eric didn't have a job so we would go junk picking for paper and metal to take to the junkyard for money. When we did this we would leave Tommy alone sleeping. Tommy slept all night and never woke up for anything until morning (I look back now, and cannot believe that we did that). I was as big as a barn but would ride the running boards of the truck so that I could hop off and go through junk, this way Eric would drive and we could cover more territory. This was how I got a carriage for the baby. We found it in the trash. There was never enough money for food or rent. My baby was born in June and he came feet first, one leg at a time. It was horrible! I screamed only one time, and that was when the doctor had to put his hand up inside of me to get at the baby's other leg and pull it down, and when I did, the doctor snapped at me to shut up! He scared the hell out of me, and I thought he was going to let me die, because it seemed like the birth had gone wrong, however, the baby and I survived, and we called him Ryan. The funny thing about this baby was that he took after my side of the family and had jet-black hair, and eyes as dark as a crow. My in-laws said that he looked like an Indian baby. My mother-in-law inferred that an Indian fathered the baby. After all, I did leave Eric when we lived in Arizona. I pointed out to her that I had Indian blood and that he was Eric's baby. His mother was such a WASP. (White Anglo-Saxon Protestant) I prefer to call her a hypocrite. Eric's mother had been married and divorced four times. We never did get to like each other.

The time came after the birth of Ryan that we couldn't afford to pay the rent. Eric found another apartment out in the country. We left our apartment in the middle of the night because we still owed the landlord rent money. The apartment that he found was actually a half a house. It had an upstairs and a downstairs. An older lady owned the house and she was very nice. I could access her half of the house through a bedroom door on my side. When Ryan was asleep and Tommy was watching Popeye, on TV, I would go over and visit with this woman. Eric was working somewhere, and was gone during the day, and I was tired of the same old same old. This was the woman that suggested that I write a book.

Eric learned how to tool leather and would make belts, handbags, and wallets to supplement his income. The time came when he was laid off his job. He had a buddy that would come over on Friday nights to play cards. Eric always won. We used to joke about his friend financing our Christmas. Between his card playing and leather crafts, things weren't bad, and we had enough food in the house and could pay our rent. Things were looking up.

One day we decided to have a little house party, and invite a few of our friends over. Eric was helping me clean the house. He was doing the upstairs, and I was doing the downstairs. Well, I had this habit of tossing my clothes onto his cedar chest at the foot of the bed and he was always bitching at me about it. I was in the kitchen and had just finished washing and drying the dishes. They were sitting on the counter next to the sink. I heard Eric come down the stairs bitching up a storm about that cedar chest. I had taken a step to the left of the sink, when, Whap! The dishwater flew up in the air and went all over my clean dishes. I turned to see what had happened, and there was Eric standing there with half of a broom in his hand. I got so pissed that I grabbed a butcher knife off the counter and started after him with it. I was yelling that if he ever tried to hurt me again that I would run the knife so far through him that he wouldn't know what happened! He fended me off with the remaining broomstick until I cooled off. He never tried to hit me again.

For some reason we decided to move back to a small town closer to the city, and Eric took an interest in racing motorcycles. What a time this would be! It seemed as though we never had money for the necessities in life, but there was always money to go out of town on racing trips. I did enjoy these trips, even though we didn't have money to spend, and the boys had a good time too. This motorcycle racing will eventually turn into a saga of it's own.

As the years went on, I noticed that Eric always managed to get what he wanted and needed, and I always came up empty. I remember one time when I was pregnant and so poor. I wanted to get something new for the baby that I was carrying, but we didn't have enough money. I almost shoplifted, but was too scared. However, Eric managed to buy what he wanted. I stood in the checkout line, fighting back the tears. I don't know if I was having a pity pot moment, or if I was pissed off. I think at that minute in time, I even hated Eric, and inside my feelings raged, but life went on, and the fickle finger of fate just kept pushing me around.

Eric found an apartment over a garage, and again didn't have a job. We were so damned poor. I remember this incident as if it happened yesterday. I had been washing our clothing and bed sheets by hand in the bathtub. I had put the bed sheets in the tub to soak. I kept my sanitary napkins in the bathroom by the side of the toilet. Well, Ryan found them and dumped the whole box into the tub with the sheets, and they were soaked. I couldn't throw them away because they cost money, so I took each one of them and put them on hangers to dry. I attached them with clothespins and hung them in the closet. My sister Kate stopped by, and when she opened the closet to hang up her coat she saw them and laughed her ass off.

I decided that something needed to be done. We needed money, and we needed food. I went out and got a job. Eric didn't object. I got a job in a factory. For some reason I needed a baby sitter. I think it was so that Eric could work on his cars and be with his friends, or look for a job. The sitter was a girl that was dating Eric's cousin so I felt that it was reasonably safe to leave her with the boys. Yeah, right! The next thing I know, Eric is in love with her! I didn't leave this time because I had the boys. I started to think about Phillip and wondered what his life was like, and if he too had gotten married. I dialed information for his number. I called. A woman answered and I hung up. I guess I was having a turn on the pity pot again. I just waited until Eric tired of this new romance, and he did, and once again he was sorry and he loved me. Boy! I was still "dumb as a box of rocks," and once again I became pregnant. Oops! I had to quit my job because the fumes were making me sick. We move again, this time to an apartment in the city.

One day I had to go to the unemployment office to sign up. While I was downtown, I decided to walk, and window shop. Of course, I couldn't buy anything because I never had any money. While walking down the street I noticed a dark skinned man following me. I ducked in and out of a few doorways to make sure. Finally, I decided to ask him why. Are you ready for this? He told me that I was beautiful, so beautiful, that I could command an army of angels! I had never in all my life been told that I was that pretty, or had any type of power. Now listen to this, he gave me his name, and wanted me to go to dinner with him. I told him that I was married, pregnant, (I wasn't showing yet), and had children and couldn't go because I wouldn't be able to get a sitter. He said that he could get a lady from his parish to sit. He was a minister, and he was from the Middle East! I told him that I would call him, and hurried home. I told Eric, but he just laughed. I looked up the man's name in the phone directory, and it turned out that he was really a minister. I had some suspicions about this man and his real intentions. I know your going to laugh at this, but I had a feeling that he was into smuggling women to his country. I figured that he lured women to his apartment, drugged them and then shipped them out. Probably rolled up in an oriental rug! It all just seemed pretty queer to me. I never did call him.

Life seemed to be getting tougher, two babies, and another on the way. Eric wasn't working, but his mother helped out a little. Our electricity was shut off, and I was really depressed. One day I sat in the kitchen on the pity pot contemplating suicide. I had thought about turning on the gas oven and killing the boys and me. Death had to be better than this. For some reason I didn't, but I had to get a job, so pregnant and all, I got one as a waitress. I didn't think that anyone would notice. I just looked like I was getting fat. However, one evening, a customer asked me when was I going to put the baby to bed. I explained to her that they were already in bed, and she indicated the one in my stomach. The jig was up. I had to quit. Now, I am fed up with everything and need to talk to someone. I wanted to leave Eric and my miserable life. I went to a mutual friend's house to discuss my situation. Eric found out that I was there and came over. He was super pissed! We got into a yelling match, and he kicked me in the stomach, however, nothing changed and I just went back home. Inside, I hated him for kicking the baby and me. A few months later I gave birth to another baby boy. He weighed over eight pounds, and the labor wasn't easy. During the last stages of labor I went into convulsions and passed out. I thought I was dying and didn't care. We named this boy Travis. By the time I went home from the hospital, the power had been restored and we had plenty of groceries. It seemed that Eric's grandmother had taken care of things, and once again I am happy. It doesn't take much does it? Well, as happy as a "box of rocks could be." I guess that if you don't expect much out of life, you don't get much. Any high expectations, or dreams that I had were buried beneath my "box of rocks" mentality.

When Travis was eight months old, we moved again and I got another job in a factory. It was on the second shift and the money was good. The work was hot, hard, fast, and I loved it. I lost all the weight from being pregnant, and was looking good. So good, that my boss started to take an interest in me. The interest never turned into anything except a hickey on my neck, because he was married. I had to take a cigarette, and burn the hickey off so I would have an explanation for Eric when he asked me about it. I told him I burned it on one of the machines I was running. Can you imagine, such horrific pain, just to cover a hickey?

I hated going home after work because I was having so much fun. I would get home after one in the morning because I had to take the bus. Travis would wake up when I came in and he would want to play. The other kids were sleeping, so I would spend a few minutes with him. He was so cute. His crib was in our room, so I would fall asleep to the sound of his baby talk.

Once again I became pregnant, but this time I had a miscarriage. I decided that it was time to take this new thing called a birth control pill. I didn't want to be pregnant anymore. I don't know what the problem was with it, but it seemed that I had a period all the time. One day Eric started screaming at me that women were dying from this pill, and that I had better stop taking it, and like a dummy, I stopped.

It always seemed that I no sooner hung the curtains, and we were moving again, or I was pregnant. This time we moved to a bigger apartment. Eric got a job working at a bakery. Life was uneventful for a short while except that I am pregnant once again, for my fourth child. And then, my kid sister Edith moved in, and hell and mayhem took over. She had been in a foster home where she was treated like a princess and given everything that her little heart could desire, but that wasn't enough, and for some reason she didn't want to live there anymore, so I let her move in with us.

What a mistake that was! She didn't lift a finger to help me with the kid's or the housework, and would stay out late at night. Sometimes she didn't bother to come home at all, and there was hanky panky going on right under my nose, and I didn't suspect a thing. You would think that by now I would be an expert at reading the signs and getting the message. The bells were going off everywhere, but I didn't, until the day that I had to go to the Laundromat. The message must have been in code, because I still didn't suspect anything. Eric took me and dropped me off. For once Edith was watching the kid's until Eric got back. When I finished the laundry I called Eric to come and pick me up. Everything seemed fine, until I walked into our bedroom. The bedspread was messed up. My little boy Tommy was behind me, when I asked what had happened to the bed. I thought that maybe the kid's had been jumping on it. Tommy said, "no mommy, daddy and Aunt Edith were playing". Because Edith was my sister, I didn't give it another thought. There was an incident when Edith had a phone call that upset her, and she went running into the bathroom crying. Eric was right behind her to comfort her. I was pissed because he never gave me that kind of attention, but again, I never suspected a thing. Dumb dumb dumb!

Edith would take off for days at a time, and I had no idea where she was, and by now, didn't care. One evening my sister-in-law called. I was sitting on the couch talking with her when a knock sounded on the kitchen door. Eric was working on something at the kitchen table, so he answered it. Lo and behold! It was my sister. I yelled for her to get out, and got my fat pregnant self up off the couch. It was only a few steps to the kitchen doorway. She was taking her coat off. Eric told her that she had better leave. She said that if anyone was going to leave, it was going to be me! I couldn't believe it! I headed for her, and at the same time Eric grabbed her and her coat, and shoved her out the door. Once outside the door, she started yelling and screaming. And get a load of this! She was screaming that she was going to fix Eric. She was going to tell everyone that the baby she was carrying was his! Holy shit! I couldn't believe it! And there I was, pregnant myself! When I confronted Eric about it he said it wasn't true, and

I, being "dumber than a box of rocks" was inclined to believe it. Jackie, the woman down stairs had been asleep with her husband when she was awakened by the ruckus. Her husband wanted to get up and come upstairs to put a stop to it before anyone got killed (his words.) Jackie told him to get back in bed. She said that it was better that we should get killed than him. (Her words.)

One day Edith called to tell Eric that he was the father of a baby boy, and that he looked just like him. He talked to her for a minute and then hung up. He told me why she called. She was giving the baby up for adoption and she just wanted to let him know. He could have cared less, and now I believe that they did mess around, and that she did have his baby. Look how damned long it took for the message to get through. For some reason I never brought the subject up, I just let it go. I had enough problems, and yes, I forgave my sister, and today we are friends.

In January I gave birth to my first daughter. We named her Jamie. She only weighed in at seven pounds and ten ounces. While I was carrying her, the doctor told me that I had to lose weight. He didn't know that my diet consisted of chocolate cream pies, brownies, and hermits. That was about all we had to eat, because Eric brought it home from the bakery where he worked. The doctor said, that if I kept gaining weight I was going to die, so the night I went into the hospital I wouldn't get into the bed. I just kept pacing, and pacing. Finally a nurse came and ordered me to get in the bed before I had the baby on the floor. I told her that I was afraid to, because of what the doctor had said. She told me that it was just foolishness, and not to worry. Everything turned out okay, and of course I didn't die, or I wouldn't be writing this book.

It seemed as if we never had real food, until Eric bought a freezer plan. What a joke that was. When you purchased a freezer it came packed with the meats, vegetables and frozen fruit of your choice. When you started to get low on your freezer you could refill at a real discount. Eric ordered all kinds of meat, fruits, and vegetables, one time, and when they ran out, he never ordered anymore because we didn't have the money, and then he sold the freezer, because we were broke. It was a long time before we ever ate that well again. Eating all that great food must have made me more fertile than ever, because, I am pregnant again, and Jamie is only six weeks old! I couldn't believe it! Again, and so soon! What was I going to do? I thought for sure that my period was just late, so I took boiling hot baths, but it didn't work, and this would be baby number five. It seemed like every time I turned around and blinked, I was pregnant, and like duh...how did that happen? For sure, the lights were on, but nobody was home.

Once again things were looking up. Eric quit the pie place, and went into construction and remodeling.

He decided that it was time to build our own home, so one evening we sat down and designed our own house. It would have five good sized bedrooms, an office, one and a half baths, a huge kitchen with big windows, and a large living room with a field stone fireplace, and two picture windows. There would also be a sunken foyer at the entrance, with a ceramic tile floor. Both bathrooms would have ceramic tiled baths and floors. The master bath had a double sink vanity with a pull out laundry chute that went right into the laundry room downstairs beneath the bathroom. All the rooms were to be connected by intercoms, with the master controls being in the kitchen. The kids would have their own playroom downstairs in the cellar. It would be heated, and the floor would be tiled, and they could write on the walls if they wanted to. It would be quite a dream house.

Eric found a piece of land high on a hillside in the country. The owner sold it to us real cheap because he said that no one would be able to build a house there. It was at the end of the road, and Eric would also build two other homes on that same road. One of them would be for his best friend and his wife and two girls. This was a new beginning, and with my pregnant assed self, I helped him dig the footings for the house. Eric finished the cellar and we moved into it until the upstairs was completed. The house was ready to move into before my fifth baby was born, and it was beautiful! Everything was so shiny and new, and I was determined to keep it that way.

When my mother-in-law first saw it, she felt that I would need a maid to help me keep it up. Yeah, right. However, everyone that came to visit us always remarked on how you wouldn't know that there were children living there because it was always so neat and clean. Of course, that was all I had to do all day, and now there were five kids. My fifth baby was another boy, and we called him Matthew. His birth was uneventful, and he was a good baby. However, I had so many hemorrhoids from this last birth that I was in tremendous pain. I was barely able to walk, and sometimes would have to crawl on my hands and knees to get around. It didn't matter to Craig. I was on my own.

The one thing that I have forgotten to mention is the fact that Eric was a lousy father. He never helped me with feedings or changed a diaper. He felt that he couldn't have anything to do with them until they were old enough to walk and talk. Whenever I had to go to the hospital to give birth, someone else would watch the kids. The only helpful thing that he would do was to make sure that everything was exceptionally clean when I came home from the hospital with a new baby.

When Matthew was six weeks old, he became very sick. I tried my best to take care of him, but his illness was beyond my knowledge. He was running a very high fever. I was continuously wiping him down with cool water and alcohol. Nothing seemed to be working, and then he started to have convulsions. I got scared and told Eric that we had better take him to the emergency room. He told me to call my brother and have him take us. It was a good thing that I took him when I did because the doctor said that if I had waited any longer, Matthew would have died. He had spinal meningitis. I called Eric and told him what was going on, I thought that he would come to the hospital but he said that it would be a waste of his time as there was nothing he could do. During the two weeks that Matthew was hospitalized, Eric only came to visit once. I guess one of the reasons was that he couldn't get a baby sitter to watch the other four kids, but I really think that he didn't want to be bothered.

Eric had a friend that lived close by. His name was Mike. He was working second shift at a factory, so every afternoon I would ride with him to the hospital. He would drop me off and pick me up after he got out of work. I would spend eight hours with Matthew. It was a terrible experience because there was nothing I could do to help him, at least I was there, but I was alone.

Being in the pediatric ward made me think. Just two floors above, I had given birth, with no idea that there were sickly babies being born too. I just naturally thought that all babies were born healthy and loved. Boy, was I "dumb as a box of rocks," or what? Day after day I watched poor little helpless babies fight to stay alive. Very few babies had visitors every day. Some had no visitors at all. One baby girl was so sick that her family didn't even bother to come and see her. They abandoned her because the illness was more than they could cope with. One day I came in and she wasn't there. I think she had died. I didn't ask, because I didn't want to know. I wanted to believe that she had been moved to another room and was getting better. Reality is such a bitter bitch.

Matthew recovered and I brought him home to the joy of his brothers and sister. We were all together once again, and everything seemed to be going fine, at least I thought it was. While I was riding back and forth to the hospital with Mike we had a lot of conversations. You aren't going to believe the revelation that was revealed to me in one of these conversations. I was telling Mike how I happened to marry Eric. I told him how he had cried. You will not believe this, but his friend told me that at one time when they were younger, Eric had cried once. It was when Mike had a girlfriend, and Eric wanted her. Eric turned on the tears, and ended up with Mike's girlfriend! I couldn't believe it. The very same trick he used on me! Now, I really hated him, but life went on, and I was fat.

I decided to go on a starvation diet. I would just drink tea and bouillon. This was not easy, as I had to cook for everyone else. I formulated a plan. I would eat with the family, and then I would go into the bathroom, put my finger down my throat, and force myself to vomit. Me, who hated to throw up!

But, I was desperate to lose weight; I hated the way I looked, especially in a bathing suit. When I look back, I can see that I wasn't really fat at all. It was all in my head, that, and Eric was always looking at other women which made me feel like I was ugly and lacking in the looks department.

As time went by I got over the trick Eric had used on me to get me to marry him. I was reasonably happy, or at least I thought I was. I had a beautiful house and five beautiful children. Sometimes I felt like one of the kids, especially when Eric brought home the groceries. We would all go running to see what he bought. He did the grocery shopping so it was a surprise. My life consisted of taking care of the kids and the house. I had no extracurricular activities and I didn't drive a car. Oh, I had a permit, but never went for my license, until just before our divorce.

Eric was racing his motorcycle, and spending time away from home. He started to hang out with a different bunch of guys who had a twisted lifestyle. A couple of the guys were married, but most of them seemed to be single. I became a good friend with one of the wives and we would discuss everything from soup to nuts. Eric had bought a Polaroid camera. He told me that it was so he could take before and after pictures of jobs that he was doing, and I believed him, again.

One day one of the wives of another biker called me up to chat. I had talked to her before at the races. Her name was Kelley. Eventually our conversation turned to Eric's purchase of the camera. She told me that the real reason Eric bought it was so that he could take nude pictures of me! I was shocked! Kelley also told me that she overheard the guys talking about their escapades away from home when they were racing. It seemed that they had been buying the service of prostitutes! I decided to start snooping through Eric's office to see if I could find any evidence to back up Kelley's allegations. In my search I came across some magazines about something called The Velvet Underground. I didn't have a clue. I started thumbing through one. Well, let me tell you! It was filled with what would become, to be called, smut. I don't think there was a word for it back then, other than dirty. There were all these ads for people interested in "Greek and French Culture" (which, I thought meant art, music and food). There were also ads where men were looking for other men, women, looking for other women, couples looking for other couples, and people looking for people interested in threesomes, foursomes, and whips and chains! Wow! This blew my mind. I couldn't believe that this kind of stuff really went on. I couldn't understand why Eric had these magazines. Now I know, but back then I was clueless. I didn't say anything to Eric right away. I wanted to sort this out in my mind and figure out what I was going to do about it.

The next night after Eric and the kids went to bed, I decided to go snooping some more, so I went down cellar into the part where he did his carpentry. I found a big barrel and opened the lid. There was some clothing, and then I hit pay dirt! I found a picture of him in all HIS naked glory! I was shocked! Someone had to take this picture! But, who, where, and why? I was so pissed that I went down into the garage, opened the door, and took the truck, and I didn't even have a driver's license! I didn't even know where I was going! All I knew was that I needed to get away from this mess! There was a storm raging and it fit my mood. I drove nowhere in particular, just around, but I needed to talk to someone so I went to Eric's Aunt Jean's house, and woke her up. It was like two in the morning and Uncle John was asleep. Thank goodness! I told Aunt Jean about Eric's new lifestyle and friends. I also told her about the picture. She didn't seem to be shocked at all, and very calmly told me that, that was how men were. I couldn't believe her attitude about it because she was a devout Christian! A real WASP! Just like my mother-in-law! She told me to go home and forget the whole thing. Well, I went home and Eric was up. He discovered that I had left, and called the radio stations to put out an appeal for me to come back home, and that he loved me. One problem, I didn't have the radio on, and I didn't care that he loved me. However, he did manage to explain everything away, and once again, I swallowed the lie. When I think back, I swallowed it because what else could I do, and where could I go with five children? Nowhere.

Eric was now spending an awful lot of time away from home, with his friends. One night he informed me that we were going to go to a house party. We called a sitter and away we went. I didn't know half the people that were there, and I wasn't comfortable with what I was seeing. Women were sitting on men's laps and necking. The problem being, the laps didn't belong to their husbands. I wanted no part of this, so I went into a bedroom and lay down. I was really confused. Allen came in and asked me what was wrong. I told him that I wanted to go home, and that I didn't like what was going on. He was angry and told everyone that I wanted to leave. On the way home I mentioned what I had seen going on at the party, and he told me that I needed a psychiatrist because I was such a prude! Can you believe that? Me? Need a psychiatrist? Not! Now when I look back, I really did, but not because I was indignant over the activities that were going on at the party, but because I was as "dumb as a box of rocks". And no matter what messages were being sent, or how many red flags were being sent up, I still wasn't getting it.

Sometime after this episode Eric approached me about playing switch. Now, I had heard rumors that people were switching husbands and wives and having sex, but I didn't believe such a thing was really happening, and I couldn't believe that Eric was asking me to do this, when I didn't even like sex! Except when I got high on alcohol, and then I was as loose as a goose, and didn't mind it. Eric discovered this one time after I had a glass or two of Blackberry Brandy, so whenever he wanted a good time, he would pry me with a few drinks. When he asked me to play switch I told him to find another bitch to switch, because this one wasn't going to go along with it.

Eric and I were doing nothing together anymore. He was always gone, and I was always stuck home with the kids. One day I told him that if he didn't start taking me out, that I would find someone who would, and I wouldn't sneak around either. I would tell him to his face, and it finally happened. I had a girlfriend who was also married and not too happy in her marriage. She called and asked me if I wanted to go to a fashion show with her. I said yes. I got dressed up, and away we went. Eric said that it was okay for me to go, but he had his own reasons for saying yes. He had his own agenda. I found out later that his best friend's wife would sneak through the woods between our houses and she and my husband would engage in sex. And in our very own bed! What an insult! Anyway, we went to the fashion show, and then after that we went out for a drink. While we were out we met two men. They were older and very distinguished looking and handsome. We went to a race track where the gentleman I was with placed a few bets for me, because I didn't know the first thing about race horses, (no, I didn't win). After the races they took us to a Polynesian Restaurant. It was very beautiful and exotic. I had a drink that had a flower floating in it. The whole evening was so enchanting, almost like a dream. I realized that I was missing out on life...the good side.

When I returned home from my evening out, I told Eric all about it. All he said was that he would like to strangle me. Things were really beginning to unravel. Somehow, I met a cute guy. His name was Eli. He had a wife, and he was unhappy with her and his life. We became friends, and Eric started to date Eli's wife. The next thing I knew, we decided to get a divorce. It was very amicable, and there was no arguing or fighting. He even bought me a car before I flew off to get a Mexican divorce. (I had managed to finally get a driver's license). When we were discussing the divorce, neither one of us gave one thought as to how the kids would feel about it, we never considered their feelings, all we knew was that we didn't see eye to eye and wanted out of this partnership. Sometimes I wonder if I didn't divorce him, and just put up with his bullshit until the kids were older, would things have been better for the kids? Or me? Who knows?

When we finally decided on the divorce we both retained the same attorney. The lawyer couldn't get over how well Eric and I got along, and couldn't understand why we would want a divorce. Of course he didn't know the real reasons, only that we had irreconcilable differences.

I flew to a Texas border town where I met my Mexican divorce lawyer. It was my first time on a Jet Airliner and I was excited beyond belief. I was on one hell of an adventure, and I loved every minute of it! I stayed at a great hotel that offered Limousine service. I would have the Limo take me to a riding stable, and then come and pick me up. I went partying every night. One evening I had too many Margaritas'. I was picked up by a Bell Hop that worked at the hotel. I was so plastered! We went to his place, which was a room in some kind of a rooming house for men. He had a bathroom, dresser and a bed. I sat on his bed, and my head was spinning. I was beginning to think that this guy wanted me to pass out so that he could rob me or rape me. I was trying very hard to think straight. The guy offered me a pillow. I refused. We made small talk, and I think he realized that there was no way that I was going to pass out so that he could take my money or anything else. He decided to take a shower. While he was in the shower I tried to look around without moving. I noticed that there are a lot of pictures on his dresser, and I remember thinking that he wouldn't try to rape me in front of those pictures. It would be a sacrilege. The guy was a Catholic too. There was a picture of The Sacred Heart hanging on his wall, so I felt reasonably safe. He wouldn't rape me, but he might rob me. Lucky me, I didn't get raped or robbed. (After all these years I still cannot figure out why he didn't do one or the other). After his shower we left. While going down the stairs I noticed that there were only men in the lobby, and that they were looking at me with quizzical looks on their faces. Like, what the hell is she doing here? My escort returned me to the hotel, and asked me not to mention the fact that he had been with me. I think it was against hotel rules, or he didn't want them to know he was trying to date, seduce, or rob, the female patrons. Who knows?

The whole Mexico trip was exciting too. We had to go across the border to finalize our divorces. I say we, because there were several of us staying at the hotel for the same reason, so we all went together. I was excited! This was another adventure! And into another country! I never gave two thoughts as to what I was doing there. I was just having one hell of a good time, and I wanted to see everything. I saw some Gypsies on a street corner, and I wanted to go with them to their camp, however, no one wanted to go with me, and it wasn't safe to go alone. I did manage to go into some of the shops and buy mementos for everyone back home. You would have never known that I was getting divorced; you would have thought that I was on vacation. After the divorce, it was time to leave and head back home. And a whole new adventure is about to begin. I am twenty- seven years old.

The kids are glad to have me back, and I am happy to see them. Eric had met a woman with six kids and was going to move in with her. Ryan was a handful so I let him go with his father. Eric, Ryan, and his new woman, and all her kids moved to Idaho, and now I had to do something to make a living. Eric was supposed to send me support money for the kids, but in all the time he was gone I only received one check.

I found a job in a factory. It was on the first shift. Because I lived in the country, I would have to get up at five in the morning to get the kid's dressed, feed, and take them to the sitters, which was down the road from me. It was an older couple and they had two children of their own. I paid them sixty dollars a week to watch my four kids. I would pick them up after work, and bring them home. With the arrival of winter, the baby sitter suggested that I leave them at her house rather than drag them out into the cold, so early in the morning. I took her up on the idea, and every night after work I would stop in at her house and spend a few hours with them. I never showed up empty handed. I always brought cookies, fruit, or candy for all the kids, including the sitter's two. If it wasn't snowing or too cold I would bring them home with me and then send them to her before bedtime. All the time I thought that this couple was kind and loving. They were not. Eric had come back from Idaho and stopped by to see the kids while I was at work. They told him of the abuse that they had suffered at the hands of the sitter and her husband. He didn't take them back there, but kept them with him until I returned from work. Everything went crazy. He decided to keep them and take over the house, as I wasn't able to keep up the payments on my salary. He said that I could have them back when I found a place of my own.

I ended up moving in with Eli's family. I thought that I was madly in love with Eli, and we would get married and live happily ever after with my kids. Eli's family was very understanding of my predicament, however, they weren't too happy with our relationship because I was a divorcee, and their son wasn't divorced yet, and I was a few years older than he was. Things worked out and they really liked me. His grandparents were the perfect old couple. They were in their eighties. The old man worked his farm, and his wife just kept house and did the cooking. The thing that struck me the most was that the wife always dressed in dresses and even wore jewelry every day. I had never seen anything like this before.

As time went on, Eli grew distant and I suspected that he had another girlfriend, and I took up drinking. Every night after work I would stop at a gin mill on my way home and I would get blind drunk! One time I was so drunk that I hit a guardrail, and cut the right fender open on my car, and passed out at the wheel. Eli came along and found me. He was pissed! He managed to wake me up and I drove home while he followed behind me. Sometimes he would go out at night and leave me with his parents. Once in awhile I would iron a shirt for him to wear when he went out.

One night his mother brought to my attention the fact that I was doing this while he was going on a date with someone else. Eli was in the bathroom shaving. I went in and confronted him about his sneaking around. He explained to me that when he first started dating me, that he loved me, however, his love was like a water faucet and he could turn it on and off whenever it behooved him to do so. I was so angry and hurt, that I slapped him and pushed him into the bathtub. His mother and father came running to see what had happened. They looked, and never said a word. I think that they new he deserved it. That night I spent the whole evening in my room crying my stupid heart out. I thought I was going to die, I really did, my heart hurt so bad. What a dummy!

I ended up leaving Eli, and moved in with my sister Kate and her husband. My sister and I worked in the same factory along with our brother Bill. Kate's husband worked nights so she and I had a good time together. All three of us had discovered diet pills. We were using them for the energy they would give us, and at the same time we were all losing weight. Kate and I would get home after work and dance for hours in her living room, or she would fix my hair so I could go out on a date. I had lost so much weight that my boobs were reduced from big, to a 32A.

One time a bunch of us from work went on a fishing derby. I wore my bikini bathing suit. The only problem was, I didn't have enough to fill the top, so I stuffed it with facial tissues. Something happened that caused me to jump, or fall into the lake, and when I did, all the tissue came floating out of my top. The girls were in the boat laughing their asses off. I couldn't get back into the boat right away because some of the guys we worked with were nearby in their boats. What a day that was! Eventually this good time was brought to an end by a fire in my sister's home.

She and I were at work when a call came in for her to go home. When she arrived, she was met by her husband, and the local fire department. Her house was a disaster. We could no longer stay there until it was remodeled, so we all moved in with some friends from work.

I think I was the first person in our city to wear mini skirts. Cars would stop to look, and hold up traffic while the guys gawked. I loved all the attention. I was looking good and knew it. At the company dances my sister and I were both in demand. We were never able to finish a drink because we were always on the dance floor. The guys called me "Go Go Tiger". They pinned this name on me because when I operated my machine, I danced. I wore a transistor radio with a headset while I worked. The maintenance man even painted tiger stripes on my *oil box. I was having a good time! And then, I met another guy.*

His name was Joshua and he was gorgeous and smelled good, and I was in love again, but still wasn't thrilled with the sexual aspect of the relationship. I would go through the motions and make all the noises that would make him feel wonderful. I acted so well that I drove him to temporary impotence. Just before he stopped seeing me, we had gone to a motel to get it on. No amount of petting would stir him up, and all he did was pace. He had something big on his mind, and it wasn't me.

Joshua was separated from his wife and kids and was considered fair game. He and I became an item, but he was also fickle. Joshua and I were madly in love with each other, I thought. The next thing I knew, he was sneaking around with a girl from the office and she was fat! And blonde! This revelation broke my heart, once again. Would I never learn?

This time I was so devastated that I tried to commit suicide. I don't think it was just my newest heartbreak that drove me to this, but a culmination of everything that was going on in my life at the time. I had been taking some tranquilizers to calm my jangled nerves. I decided to take all that I had left, and sleep myself into the arms of death. I took them and went out to my car. I closed the windows, and locked the doors, and then I started the engine. I was beginning to feel the effects of the pills, and I started to fall asleep, down into a warm soft, fuzzy world where there was no pain, no confusion, no lost loves, or broken families, only peace. The feeling was wonderful, and I was not afraid. Soon, from what seemed to be far away, I heard a pounding with a muffled voice; it was my older brother Bill. Somehow he managed to figure out what I was trying to do, and he wanted me to open the car door. He was yelling my name, and the longer and louder he yelled, the more he pulled me back. I didn't want to come back. I wanted to stay in that warm peaceful place, but he wouldn't let me. He wouldn't stop yelling, and pounding. Finally, in my drugged stupor I reached up and unlocked the door. He reached in and pulled me out of my car. It was cold outside, and I wanted to be warm and go to sleep. My brother wouldn't let me. He shoved me into his car and drove all over with the windows open, trying to keep me awake. At one point he stopped long enough to grab a sandwich and coffee. He force fed me to keep me awake. After driving around for several hours, he felt that I was past death so he took me home. I slept for three days, only getting up long enough to get a drink and go to the bathroom. I had missed work also, but my sister covered for me, as we worked together. I was beginning to learn that all men were ass holes, but the lesson was taking a long time to sink in, and even then it never quite sunk in all the way. I think it just skipped around on the surface of my mind.

Things in my life went from bad to worse. Eric had lost the house to the bank, and his girlfriend moved back in with her husband temporarily. Why, I don't remember. Eric had the kids and he needed someone to watch them while he worked. He came to me and offered me a deal. I get to stay with the kids, and watch them while he works. This way I had a place to live, I'm with the kid's, and he will watch them during the day, while I work. This was all fine and good, except when I got home from work, there would be dirty dishes, and the house would be a mess. I had no clue what he did all day, as he worked second shift. The next thing I know he couldn't watch them during the day and found a sitter. The next thing I knew I was moving out of the apartment, because I couldn't afford the rent, and pay a sitter too. The kid's ended up living with the sitter. She was really super nice and treated the kid's as if they were her own, but her husband was an asshole, and he would complain about how much they ate. Her husband and I would eventually have a run in.

I had to work two jobs in order to be able to pay for the sitter, buy their clothing, and any other needs they might have had, including myself. I didn't live with them, as there wasn't enough room, so I had a room in the house of a co-worker. All I did was work. I would be to work at the factory by seven in the morning. At three thirty I would go home, shower, press my waitress uniform, and get to my second job by five o'clock, where I would sometimes have to work until four and five in the morning. Working two jobs started to take its toll. At the factory I would be falling asleep on the assembly line, and on my lunch I would go lay down on the couch in the ladies room and take a nap. The funny thing was, that I was putting the parts together, but because I was half asleep, I wasn't doing it right. My sister was at the end of the line taking my units apart to repair them. People use to call it our job security. When I got off my second job I would sometimes fall asleep in the car while I was waiting for it to warm up. My co-worker became concerned because on my days off, all I did was sleep. I didn't want to be a bother to her anymore so I moved out, and got a room at a hotel in the city. I would be so tired that I would have the night desk clerk give me a wake up call at six in the morning. One cold November morning after I had left my second job I had asked the clerk to call me at six. It was already three in the morning. I sat on the edge of the bed thinking, and I was so tired. The next thing I knew, my phone was ringing. It was my sister, and she wanted to know how come I wasn't at work that day. I asked her what time it was. She told me that it was four o'clock in the afternoon. I was flabbergasted! I called the desk, and asked them why they hadn't given me my wake up call. The clerk said that he did, but when he received no answer, he thought I had already left.

I was so busy that I had no time for men, until one day, into the restaurant walked an Army Sergeant with another soldier. They sat in my section. The sergeant had the biggest, brownest, saddest eyes I had ever seen, and he was as cute as a button. I was immediately drawn to him. I gave him my number at the hotel and we started to date, when I could take a night off.

My sister had been listening to a radio contest where you had to go out and about town looking for a missing letter to a word. She talked me into taking a night off work to go with her to look for this missing letter. While we were out snooping around in the dark, we were pulled over by two State Troopers. They were gorgeous! One of them shone his flashlight on my legs, and liked what he saw. He asked me for a date, and my phone number. I said, yes, and gave him the phone number of my hotel.

At this time in her life my sister Kate was not happy with her husband or happy in her marriage. She thought that my life was exciting and wanted to be a part of it, so she left her husband and moved into the hotel with me. I am dating the Army Sergeant, and Kate is dating his buddy. We are having a good time. The Sergeant becomes my steady boyfriend, but when he went home on a weekend I would see the State Trooper. The Trooper was a country boy, and didn't know the first thing about women, and he had just joined The State Police Department. Because he was so naïve he thought I was the greatest thing since mashed potatoes, and I loved the way he made me feel special, and beautiful, but I wasn't in love with him. I liked him a lot, but I was in love with The

Sergeant. There is the word that is every woman's downfall. LOVE.

After awhile I came to the conclusion that love has nothing to do with sex, and everything to do with the heart. I say this because even though I was in love, I only went through the motions of sex and never derived any feelings from it. I just did it, and doing it with my Sergeant wasn't a big chore. I liked the closeness of the sex act with him. One problem, I became pregnant, as if this was something new. My God! Where was my head! When he found out, he was pissed! He insisted that it wasn't his, and I insisted that it was. He had been married twice before, and neither of his wives ever became pregnant, so he just assumed that he was shooting blanks. He wanted me to have an abortion, and I didn't, because I didn't believe in it. When he was sober our relationship was strained, but when he had a few drinks, he was wonderful.

Kate, and our older brother Bill bought a new house trailer together, and we moved out of the hotel, and in with him. The trailer was beautiful, and we each had our own bedroom. We divided everything three ways, so it wasn't expensive. When we first moved in, I wasn't pregnant, and Kate and I were still having fun.

Because of the shooting of a State Trooper, Kate and I ran into a roadblock one night after having been out to a dance. The Troopers were so nice that we decided to go and buy donuts and coffee for them. Well, Kate met a cutie and they saw each other a couple of times. It didn't last long because the guy had a wife, and Kate didn't know it until one night when the guy's wife called to see whose number she had found in his pocket. Kate was cool and told the woman that it was her brother's phone, and that they probably knew each other. One of the fun things about meeting all these Troopers was that we were able to speed when we had to go to work. They would pull us over, see who it was, and then tell us to be careful and slow down. Yeah, right.

My sister and I had a lamp with a red light bulb in it. It sat on the counter beneath the kitchen window, but most of it could be seen from outside. Our brother had a fit about it and said that it looked like we were running a whorehouse. It was funny because that was how the Troopers would find their way to the trailer to have coffee, and we had a lot of Troopers in and out. It was all on the up and up. We just had all these great guys stopping by for coffee when they were on duty. One time two of them even helped to put some toys together for my kid's for Christmas. They were friends, and no more than that, but our brother made us stop having them over because he said it didn't look right, that, and the red light in the window. Our life started to become dull, and then one day Kate and I had slid off the highway in a snowstorm. We were on our way home from work when we slid off the road and into a ditch. A tractor-trailer stopped, and this cute hunk of a guy got out. He offered to help get us out of the ditch, which he did. Then he and Kate became an item for a short time, a very short time, because he was traveling on the southern coast of the states, and wasn't able to get up here and see her. Kate was becoming really bored because, I, now being pregnant, didn't want to run around anymore, so she ended up going back with her husband, and she too became pregnant.

Because I had what I considered a home, I had my daughter Jamie come to live with my brother and me. For the first time in a long time I felt like a real mother. I kept her dressed like a little princess, and when she played outside she never got dirty. Now mind you, I am pregnant and looking like I am just gaining weight, and my brother doesn't even notice. One day the tractor- trailer driver that my sister went out with, showed up at my door. I was shocked. I told him that Kate had gone back with her husband. He hung around for a while, and then left. A few weeks later he returned. He had brought me some fresh oranges and grapefruit up from Florida. My brother Bill baby-sat with Jamie while I went on a date with the trucker. He tried to kiss me, and I wouldn't let him. He finally asked me what was wrong. I said nothing, and he tried to kiss me again, and again I said no, and pushed him away, and then the light bulb went on in his head. He asked me if I was pregnant. I said yes. It didn't matter to him. He wanted to take Jamie and me with him to live in Florida. He said that he would take care of all of us. He didn't care that I was having someone else's baby. I told him no, that I couldn't go. I never heard from him again.

I am getting fatter, and the baby's father is seeing less and less of me. The time came when I had to move out of my brother's trailer because I didn't want to tell him that I was going to have a baby. He was old fashioned and didn't believe in having babies without being married, so I moved in with my sister Kate and her husband. About a month later, on a hot August day I had a baby boy, and I named him Luke, after his father, The Sergeant. My older brother found out, was appalled, and pissed off because I managed to hide it from him for as long as I did. My wonderful Brown eyed Sergeant transferred to a recruiting station near his hometown, and tried to forget the whole affair. When the baby was born, I called him and told him. He sent me a check for a hundred dollars to buy a crib and some baby clothes. I guess he thought that he could buy me off.

When Luke was six weeks old I took him on a bus to see his father. His father was pissed, but cooled off after he saw the baby. He looked at him and made the remark that he couldn't be his because his eyes weren't brown. I explained to him that Luke's eyes had not attained their permanent color yet. We spent the day together and then we headed back home. Luke senior always sent support money to me for Luke Jr. He never missed a payment, and if I ever needed anything, all I had to do was write and ask. He was an honorable man, and kept his word. When I needed money he sent me a check, however, I didn't ask that often.

The conditions at my sister's house were deteriorating because she was pregnant and unable to work. Jamie was still with me, and Luke, at Kate's house. Kate needed quiet so she could get her rest, as it was her first baby. She was always tired and sleepy. I was worried that Jamie would bother her so I would send her over to her friend's house to spend the day. They adored having her and always told me what a good girl she was. Things at my sister's house were tight because they had no money and couldn't really afford to have us living there. I had to make a decision, and it was one of the hardest ones that I would ever have to make. I called my ex husband and asked him if he would take Jamie to live with them for a while, because I had no way to feed her. We didn't even have any milk. I had to get a job. He said that he would take her, and then he came and got her, and things got worse.

I found a job as a meat wrapper at a grocery store. It was at the top of the hill from where I lived with my sister. It was winter, and I had no boots or shoes. All I had to wear on my feet were sandals. On my lunch hour I would trek back down the hill to check on Luke. He would be awake, but Kate would be sleeping. He was a good baby and made no demands on her, so she was able to have her naps. I knew that

I had to move, but wasn't sure what I could do, or how I would manage.

Through a friend, a woman heard of my plight and came to see me. She had a beautiful big home, husband, and three children. Her name was Sybil. She was looking for a Nanny, and someone to take care of everything while she and her husband worked. She had a large extra bedroom, and the job would include pay, room, and board, and some weekends off, and I could have Luke live there too. I jumped at the chance to be in a real home, so I took the position, and moved in. It was right down the street from my ex husband and all the kids. This was going to be great!

Well, just because the kids lived in the next block, didn't mean that I would get to see them. I didn't. Their stepmother said that I was a bad influence on them, so she wouldn't let them see me. I guess that when they were allowed to see me, they went back home with an attitude. However, my little boy Travis didn't care what his stepmother and father said. On Sunday mornings he would come down, have breakfast with me and spend the day. He was the only one that dared defy them.

My life had become pretty routine. I baby-sat, cooked, cleaned, did the laundry and grocery shopped. The woman I worked for always gave me a blank check when I went grocery shopping. The only time she cooked was on weekends, and then it was always something fancy. On weekends the dining room table was set with a linen tablecloth and napkins, crystal drinking glasses, and real silverware. I learned a lot from my employer. I learned about expensive clothing, entertaining, and the high-class lifestyle of people with money. I also saw child brutality, under the guise of discipline, and was shocked to see it taking place in a wealthy, Catholic household. I felt bad for the kids, but they didn't seem to be affected by it. They were good kids as far as I was concerned.

One day my employer's husband sat down and had a talk with me about how important it was for me to find a man with money. All I wanted was a man to love me, and to hell with money! Boy! Was I "dumb as a box of rocks," or what? There is a lot to be said for money, and nothing to be said for love, but as usual, I was clueless. Today, I would rethink that idea. My grandmother once said, "that it was just as easy to love a rich man as it was to love a poor one." She was right, and I was dumb. Today, I would definitely go for the money, and to hell with the love.

One day, just before Valentines Day, Sybil and her husband gave me a card. In it were the plane reservations for a flight to Vermont and a two-day stay at a nice hotel. I was to take Luke to see his father! I waited until just before I left and then I sent Luke Sr. a telegram to tell him that I would be arriving with the baby. This way he couldn't talk me out of it. When we arrived at the airport *his father was there to pick us up. He was happy to see us, but was dismayed that I had not called to tell him that we would be coming. It seems as though his second wife left Poland to come to the states to be with him. He was not happy with her. All she wanted to do was party every night and he was too tired from having worked all day. However, he wasn't angry with me, so one day I left him with the baby and went to a mall that was across from the hotel. When I returned to the hotel, he was on the bed with the baby having a good time. He was smiling and laughing, and I really felt at that time that there was a good possibility that we would end up together. Dumb! Dumb! Dumb! He knew that I had been married before and that I also had five kids, but it didn't seem to bother him, and we never discussed them. He had met Jamie though, and he liked her. He called her "Beans" because that is what her nickname was, and he always asked me about her. For some reason I had imagined the six of us as a family, but that was a stretch of my imagination, a really big stretch. I never had my thinking cap on straight. I was always a romantic. What a waste of time! What a dreamer! What a Dork! Bah, humbug!*

Through the newspaper I started to write to an American Indian who was a Green Beret. His name was Kip. He looked like Trini Lopez, well, his picture did, but in person he didn't. We wrote several letters back and forth. We decided that I should fly to Fort Bragg to meet him. My employer watched Luke so I could go, and I had the time coming. I had saved some money, so I flew down South to meet him. Boy! What a shock! I was looking at all these tall, handsome men, trying to find him, when all of a sudden this little short guy came up to me. He was cute, but he was so short! Not much taller than I. It took me awhile to get over the shock that he wasn't tall, dark, and handsome, but, short, dark, and handsome with a brush cut!

He turned out to be a lot of fun, and he made me feel special. He took me to a dance at the base. I had never seen so many men in one place in all my life. It was an ugly girl's paradise! When we were dancing some guy bumped into us, and he promised me that if it happened again that he would lay the guy out. We had sex, but it was nothing to get excited about, not for me anyway. He enjoyed it, and even complimented me on my performance. Said I was the best this side of the ocean. Whoop-tee-do! I did it because I felt that it was the thing to do, so again, I went through the motions. What a drag! Every other aspect of my vacation was great. The time was too short though, and I had to get back home to Luke, and my job. The best part of this whole scene was the flying. I loved being in the air.

Life was going along smoothly, and the time had come for me to take another trip to Fort Bragg, only this time I didn't let my guy know I was coming. I wanted it to be a surprise. I took a cab from the airport to my hotel. When I got out of the cab, I was surrounded by men! Lots of gorgeous, hunky men! And they all wanted to carry my suitcases to my room. I ended up carrying my own suitcases because I didn't want to have to make a choice.

As soon as I got to my room I put in a call to my boyfriend. He wasn't there so I left a message. I no sooner hung up the phone and it started ringing. It was all those men I had seen when I arrived, and they all wanted to go out with me! There was no way! I was there to meet my guy! During all these phone calls my boyfriend was trying to get through to me. When he finally did, he was hopping mad, (He had his nerve) but he cooled off fast. I just told him the truth. Later that evening he was able to get off the base and take me to dinner. The next day he called me to tell me that he couldn't get away, but would be sending a buddy of his to take me out and spend time with me. (Little did I know that he had a wife, and that she was also in town.) The buddy showed up, and he was a hunk! He looked like Steve McQueen, and he was tall. We went out and had a really good time. He was a perfect gentleman, and there was no hanky panky. At the time I was thinking how much I would like to have this guy as my boyfriend.

This trip was a real bummer as I wasn't able to spend as much time with Kip as I would have liked to. I ended up leaving Fort Bragg two days earlier than I had planned. I decided to stop off in Washington D.C. for a while as I had never been there. I went to the Smithsonian Institute and walked around and looked at the different monuments. It was a real bore because there was no one to share the experience with. My flight back home turned out to be a wild ride because of an electrical storm, and I loved it!

Life back in my hometown was slow and boring. I wrote to Luke's father and kept him up to date on Luke Jr. He was sending sixty dollars a month, and continued to do so until Luke turned twenty-one. On weekends I would go out with my girlfriends. In fact, one of them was my ex-husbands second wife. Somehow she and I had gotten beyond our misunderstandings of each other, and became pretty good friends. One Saturday night we went out to an Indian Bar. I was looking pretty good with my short blonde hair, and skinny looking self. I was just sitting there talking with her when she gave me a nudge, and whispered for me to look over to my left. Well, I did, and there was the tallest, most handsome Indian guy I had ever seen, and he was checking me out. I pretended that I didn't see him and kept talking to my girlfriend. The next thing I knew, a big hand was pressed gently over my mouth and this hunk of a guy was whispering in my ear that I talked too much. He introduced himself to me. His name was Craig. As the evening wore on we got to know each other, and he also got drunk. I wasn't familiar at all with this drunk stuff, and just sloughed it off as a result of partying. Craig and I took my friend home, and then Craig asked me to take him home, as he didn't have a car. He lived on the Reservation just outside of town. I knew where it was as I had spent a lot of time there. On the way, he told me that his aunt didn't like "Yellow Hairs". I thought... Oh shit, now what do I do? We arrived at his house to find that everyone was asleep. He fixed me something to eat and then I left. The following weekend we went out again. My hair was still blonde. We went to his house so I could meet his aunts, grandmother, and cousins. I was a nervous wreck, even though I am part Indian. His family was not friendly at all, and I knew it was because of the blonde hair. One aunt actually glared at me. I think at that time they were a bit prejudice. As time went on they liked me and accepted me as part of the family, and the grandmother actually thought that Craig and I would get married. This was not to be, and boy, was I glad.

I was seeing a lot of Craig, but was not in love. I think that over the years the idea of love went out the window along with any romantic notions that I had about how love should really be. I didn't believe that anything as wonderful as love should be the cause of so much emotional pain. It made no sense. I had been there and done it, and didn't want to do it anymore, so I guess you could say that Craig and I were lover's. However, I could never understand how you could be lovers when you weren't in love. I guess that was the word for sex. And, how could you sleep with someone without actually sleeping with them, when all you did was have sex, and then get up and go home? I guess the word's lovers and sleeping were used to make having sex seem acceptable. Craig and

I just had sex. There was no love to it, and most of the time I got up and went home. However, I did like the feel of all that muscle lying next to me. It always made me feel safe and secure, and that was a good feeling, until the night he popped me, and then all there was, was fear. Let me explain.

One evening Craig and I went out drinking. We picked up a buddy of his and took him along with us. Whenever we went to a different bar, I was left sitting by myself, and I began to get pissed off. By now, I have a pretty good buzz on. When we headed for the next bar, I ran stop signs, and slid through them on wet leaves. We arrived at the next bar. Craig's buddy got out of the car along with Craig. I decided that I had had enough of their shit, and started to drive off. Another car came by and temporarily stopped me from completing my getaway. At the moment I had to stop, Craig jumped back in the car. He slapped me in the face. He said that it was for speeding, and then he slapped me in the face again and told me that that was for being a bitch. I could feel the warm blood running down my chin, and I could taste the iron in it. Craig ordered me to get out of the car. He was going to teach me a lesson. I got out and figured that he was going to kill me, but I couldn't stop it. I was too stunned and had had too much to drink. I stood under the streetlight, in the rain, and when Craig saw the blood and my swelling face, he ordered me to get back in the car. He told me to head for the emergency room. His buddy came out to see where he was, and Craig told him that I was going to the hospital. His buddy went back into the bar. I didn't want to go to the emergency room, and told Craig that I would take care of myself. I was too humiliated to go anywhere. That, and my face looked like a grape that had been stomped on. He said OK. He took a paper napkin and soaked it in beer and wiped my face as I drove, and then he passed out. I drove into my driveway and parked the car. Craig's head was hanging out the window, and he was out like a light, and I left him there. Instead of going into the house, I went up the hill to my ex-husband's house. I got them out of bed and told them what had happened. Eric wanted to go and beat the crap out of Craig, but I insisted that he leave him alone and he did. Eric's wife brought out a mirror so I could take a look at my face.

I couldn't believe what I saw! It wasn't me! It was a mess! My bottom lip was split open, my left eye was black and blue as was the whole left side of my face, and it was all swollen. I couldn't believe that I let this happen to me. Any other time I would have stood my ground and fought back. This time I was drunk, and my opponent was way bigger than I. Anyway, after some small talk I went down the hill and home. I checked the car to see if Craig was still there. He was, and his head was still hanging out the window, and it had started to rain again. I wasn't about to wake him up, so I left him there, and I went in the house and got ready for bed. One thing was different this time. I took my loaded rifle to bed with me just in case Craig woke up, and thought he might pick up where he left off. I would have shot him before I let him hit me again. My sleep was fitful and I awoke early before anyone else. I went down to the kitchen and was making coffee when I heard the back door open. Craig asked me why I left him in the car all night. I could tell by the sound of his voice that he had no clue as to why I didn't wake him up to come in with me. I never said a word. I just turned around so he could see what he had done. One look was worth a thousand words. He asked me if he had done it, and I said yes. He said, "take me home". I did, and not one word passed between us. Later that day my brother-in-law stopped by to get something. He took one look and asked me what the other guy looked like. I told him I didn't want to talk about it.

I have to tell you that whenever I went out I always had a sitter for Luke, and it was my employer, and if they were out of town I hired someone to come in and watch her three children, and my one. The night that I was popped in the face, they were out of town for five days, so they never got to see my bruises.

A week had passed since my face had been rearranged. I went out one night and was sitting in one of the bars looking out the window, when I saw a car pull up and Craig got out. My stomach flip-flopped. Craig came in and sat down next to me. He said that I had healed pretty fast. I asked him why he had done it. His answer was so stupid! He said that it was because he was beginning to care too much for me. I just told him that I didn't ever want him to care that much for me again. Our relationship was slowly petering out. The end came one night when we were out jacking deer. I had gone out to the Reservation, or the rez, to visit Craig's family. While I was there Craig came by, and I ended up going with him to the apple orchards to look for deer.

In my pocket was a tiny little statue of the Infant of Prague. I was a nervous wreck, as this was against the law, and I kept rubbing this little statue for luck. I was doing the driving, and Craig was holding the spotlight so he could look for deer herds. We found one. He gave me a bunch of instructions, and I forgot half of them. I had dropped him off as per instruction. I went down the road about a quarter of a mile and turned around and headed back towards him, per instruction, or so I thought. He jumped in the car and started yelling and telling me how stupid I was, and all the time he was yelling I kept rubbing that little piece of plastic in my pocket. He had me stop the car, and hold the spotlight, as he aimed the rifle out the window right next to my ear, and bang! He shoots a deer. We got out of there fast, and made it back to the rez. On the way we ran into one of Craig's buddies, who wanted to know if we had seen anything. Craig proceeded to tell him about my stupidity and how he dropped a deer. They decided that the two of them would go back and look for the animal. And all the time I am still rubbing that statue. I just wanted off the rez and back home. That was not to be until later. Craig took me to his house, and told me to go to sleep on the couch. He was going after the deer. I didn't sleep to well, because I was worried about what might happen if he went back and couldn't find the deer. I decided that I wasn't going to wait for him. I got up and went home. I didn't see him again until I became involved in a bar brawl.

This was the seventies, and life was wild. Sex, drugs, and Rock and Roll. It was party time to the max. I didn't do drugs but managed to hang out with people that did. I had a girlfriend that did them all. One night we went out to our favorite bar together. The place was packed as usual, and you could pick out the ones that were, stoned, high, or tripping. My friend Gennie had taken something before I picked her up. By the time we got to the bar she needed something else, so she headed to the ladies room. I went with her. She took something, and was incoherent. She was leaning against the wall and started to slide down it. I grabbed her and stood her up. While I was trying to get her in an upright position, I noticed that she had a knife in her hand, beneath her poncho. I was like, oh shit! What do I do now? I quick ran out of the ladies room and grabbed her old boyfriend and pulled him back in with me. He got Gen and took her out of the bar. I went and sat at the bar. I was minding my own business, when out of the blue, Craig came over to say hello and make small talk. There was an Indian woman sitting to my right. She kept *making wise cracks about my blonde hair and false eyelashes. I am trying to ignore her and listen to Craig. The woman finally said that she was going to rip my false eyelashes right off my face. I am still ignoring her when all of a sudden, whap! She had me by the hair and bent backwards over the bar! I was like...what the hell? I reached back behind her head and grabbed a hand full of her neck and hair. I was twisting it for all I was worth. Craig jumped in, and pulled me away from her, but when he did, it was with such force that I went spinning across the floor like a ballerina, except that I wasn't as graceful, and I fell, putting a run in my nylons. I picked myself up and was brushing myself off when I saw the bitch that had jumped me. She was coming right at me! I grabbed a barstool and raised it, just as a bunch of women grabbed her and pinned her to the wall. They were yelling at her for starting the whole fracas, as I had been sitting there minding my own business. Craig came over and took the barstool from me, as I didn't need it anymore. If those women had not grabbed her, I would have brought that stool down on her head. Craig talked me into leaving the bar, which I did. Funny thing...Craig always thought that I was such a lady and above the trashy life. He was right. I was above it, however I did take a side trip every now and then, and was like everyone else I hung out with. Always drinking, and in a bar.*

I gave up my position as Nanny because my employer was complaining about my type of friends, and the fact that I spent my time off in the bars, so I left and moved in with my girlfriend who was also my former baby-sitter. She was the one with the husband that didn't like me. I got a job as a meat wrapper and she watched   Luke for me. One problem, her husband was a drunk and he would abuse her after his binges. One Easter Eve he came home drunk.   Their kids were asleep, and so was Luke. Her husband started yelling and pushing her around. I got out of bed, and went to their bedroom door where I put in my two cents. He finally shut up and left her alone. At that time I was dabbling in Witchcraft. My girlfriend's husband drove a Cadillac that was his pride and joy. One evening while he was asleep I went out and performed a spell upon his car. Two days later, he was involved in an accident. No one was hurt, but his pride and joy now had some dents in it. I don't know whether the spell worked, or if it was fate, but it happened, and I was glad. He was a jerk.

One thing I learned about witchcraft.   If you believe in it, it works. I used it against my sister's husband too. One time he had borrowed my car to haul his snowmobile. I told him that I didn't think it would work, but he used it anyway. The next thing I knew, a phone call came in from him, confirming my prediction. My car couldn't carry the weight and broke down. He apologized and told me that when he got his income taxes back that he would pay me for the car. I didn't rant and rave, but took him at his word, but he was full of shit. His tax money came and he bought all kinds of camping equipment. His neighbor told me. I was so pissed that I went and did a spell, and what do you think? A big thunderstorm blew up, and knocked down a large tree right on top of all that new camping equipment, destroying everything. I have learned a lot about witching and spells since that episode, so I don't monkey with the unknown anymore, but at the time it felt good to exact some revenge.

After work I would go to the local bar which was across from my place of employment. My girlfriend babysat so I could work. It was a popular joint and always hopping. One night I met a handsome dude from Virginia. His name was Andre. He was here in my hometown, working on a bridge. We struck up a conversation, and then started seeing each other. He was married, but I never knew it until several years later. I should have known, because on some weekends he would go home to visit his family, meaning his parents. You would think that after one cheating husband, a couple of lover's, and two boyfriends and a working brain, that I would have suspected something! But, no...I am still a trusting idiot who is "dumber than a box of rocks," with a brain on hold. Anyway, we would take Luke and go to the local park and have little picnics and talk. I would sit on the grass and Andre would lay with his head in my lap. It was like something out of a romance novel, except that I knew there was no such thing as romance. I think it was like on our second date that I went to bed with him. It was the only time that we had sex. It was just wham bam! But, what a bam it was, because the next thing

I knew, I was pregnant! I couldn't believe it! Talk about stupid! It never entered my mind that this would happen! That it could happen! Again! After six kids you would have thought that I would know what happens when you have unprotected sex, but for some reason I kept on doing it. My mind must have been on vacation, but my body got left behind! When I think about how many times I went through all of the pain of birthing, you would have thought that it would have been enough to make me at least think about getting pregnant. I really think that I must have had a subconscious need to punish myself, as all of my births were long, hard, and extremely painful. No one in their right mind would want to go through all that pain, at least, not more than once. Now I am really in a pickle! What do I do? Abortion is out of the question. It isn't even an option. I hadn't even told Andre and he had stopped seeing me. (His conscience must have been bothering him). I would leave little notes for him at his work site, but he never answered them. The next thing I knew, he was gone, and I was alone in my dilemma. What do I do?

I remembered that I had a miniature license plate with his plate number on it. This was my first encounter with the world of investigation, and I loved it. Using a few pretexts and the telephone, I soon found out where he lived, however, I didn't contact him until after the baby was born.

I couldn't stay at my girl friends house any longer because I couldn't stand her husband, so I just up and left. I was fired from my job because I locked horns with my boss, and he let me go. I had a little money that I had managed to save, so   Luke and I lived in my car for a while. We would sleep in the rest areas along the super highway. The weather was beginning to get very cold, and I was very pregnant. Luke had to sleep in his pajamas and a snowsuit to keep warm. I couldn't let the car run very long for heat because I had to conserve the gas. That, and I didn't want us to get asphyxiated. I had run out of ideas and places to go. Somehow, some way, I managed to run across my friend Sybil. With her help and welfare, I was able to get a three-room apartment. The building had just been remodeled and everything was new. It was very spacious and beautiful. I didn't have a TV or a radio so I spent a lot of time reading and playing with Luke. Another tenant moved in across the hall, and she and I became good friends. She had a son also, so he and Luke played together while we hung out. Come to find out her husband was a jerk who would get drunk and beat the hell out of her, and her boy. He didn't live with them, but he would visit once in awhile. Once, after one of his visits, Patty found a gun that he had hidden in a storage room at the end of the hall. She gave it to the police. Her husband didn't come around after that, and eventually she divorced the bastard.

I was over to Patty's apartment when my labor began. We were eating shrimp and watching TV.

When the pains became two minutes apart we called the doctor, and he told me to get to the hospital right away. I called my other girlfriend, Sybil, and she came and took me. The baby was a boy and I called him Storm. When Storm was six months old my friend Sybil asked me if I would take her two boys on a camping trip to Canada. She also had a fresh air kid from New York City, and wanted me to take her too. I wasn't going to handle all these kid's on my own, so I had another girlfriend that was much younger than I, so I asked her if she wanted to go. She said yes. Well, there were five kids, she and I, and no room left for anyone else. My friend Patty wanted me to take her boy with us, but there was no way, because with the camping equipment and the seven of us, there just wasn't any room. I think she was upset, but it couldn't be helped. One more was too many, and no room to boot. We were gone for ten days. We would have stayed longer but we ran out of money.

Early one morning my door buzzer rang. It was a security buzzer. You couldn't gain entry without my OK. Anyway, it was Luke Sr. I couldn't believe it! When the buzzer went off, I asked who it was. This voice came back at me saying, "open the door, I feel stupid standing here talking to a building". I was so excited. I let him in. It seems that he had gotten inebriated and decided to drive three hundred miles to see his son and me. He sat across the street in the parking lot most of the night, and almost left without seeing us, but decided that he had come *this far, so he might as well. He didn't stay long, but thought that his son was a little spoiled.*

Life was going along smoothly for a change, and then, wham! Out of the blue pops my ex-husband! He has a problem. He is in between girlfriends and wives, and needs me to take care of the five children that we had together. With these five, and the two I now had, made seven kids and myself, stuffed into a one-bedroom apartment. It wasn't bad, and believe it or not, the kids were great. They were also quiet because they had to be. The landlord was an attorney and his office was downstairs. If he found out that I had all these kid's in my apartment, he would have evicted me. As it turned out, Eric fixed his love life, and came for the kids. Someone in the apartment building told the landlord that I had all those kid's, and I was evicted anyway. However, I did have the time to find another apartment with two bedrooms, and another adventure begins, and I am pregnant again. I stop asking myself why, and just accept the fact. The message was no longer being sent, and I was really dumb. It was Craig's baby as I had started seeing him on and off again. More off than on, but just long enough. There was no way that I was going to tell him that I was expecting his child.

The apartment needed to be cleaned and painted. Craig's cousins came over to give me a hand. On the second day in the apartment I had a mis-carriage. I think it was a result of all the heavy lifting and the chemicals that I was using to clean with. I called my sister-in-law while I was having the expulsion pains. She helped me to get through it. It wasn't a baby per se, but a tiny thing, that I buried in the back yard. I was sad that this had happened, but I was also glad. I didn't need any more children. After this, life settled down for a while and was rather quiet and uneventful, but it didn't last for long. A girl moved in upstairs over me. She had a little boy, and we traded baby-sitting. It was party time! Across the street from me lived Kips sister Sandy, the Green Beret that I used to date. She was a barmaid at a little tavern. I would walk to this joint and hang out drinking and dancing and having a blast. The next thing I know, bam! My ex-husband is in between women again and needs my help with the kids. I say OK, and once again my apartment is full. This time I had a cellar that I was able to convert into sleeping quarters for them. The older boys, and Jamie went down the street to school. One problem, it was in a tough neighborhood, and I worried about the impact this type of school would have on them. There were fights and they brought home head lice. What a mess! And the kids all had curly hair, which made it difficult to get rid of the blasted things, but I managed.

I began to drink almost every night. I would put the kids to bed and have my girlfriend keep an eye on them, and then I would head to the bar. After closing time, Kips sister would load up a shopping bag with beer and we would go to my house and drink some more. She would stagger across the street to her house, and I would watch her stumble up the stairs, and then I would go to bed. I couldn't get up in the morning to get the boy's off to school, or watch the little ones, so I kept the second oldest home to take care them while I slept. One day, a teacher came to the house. I was in bed, hung over, but awake. I listened as she asked Ryan questions about me. She asked him if I drank. He said yes. She asked him if I got drunk. He said, not so you'd notice, " she doesn't stagger when she walks". That little episode was a wake up call. There was no way I wanted to be a drunk, so I stopped drinking at night, and limited myself to social drinking on the weekends that I would go out.

The word got back to Eric about the boys getting into fights at school, and that they had bugs, so he straightened out his love life, and once again came and got them, but before he did, he and I double dated. He was with his latest girlfriend, and I, with her brother. We all went out dancing. The reason I remember this so well is because I was wearing a wig. My date and I went outside for a breath of air. I leaned up against the building, which was rough stucco. When I stepped forward, my wig was stuck to the building! I was so mortified! And then my date reached up and pulled off his toupee! It wasn't a bad evening, but my date was rather dull. I never saw him again.

I was out one evening with some friends when they suggested that I should have a party at my house.

I didn't see anything wrong with that, because I figured that there would only be three or four of us, so the following Friday I did. I sent my two boys upstairs with my girlfriend and then the party began. And what a party it turned out to be! My house was filled with people that I knew, and some that I didn't know. Most of them were my friends from the rez. Two of the guys brought a sound system in and played music. The next thing I know, there is LSD, and pot being passed around, and I am getting very nervous. People are getting high and drunk. The music is so loud it can be heard two blocks away. The next thing I knew the cops are out in front of my house! One of my girlfriends dated cops so she went out to see what the problem was. Meanwhile, I am grabbing shit and flushing it down the toilet. Some people were so stoned that they were mesmerized by the flashing red lights on the police cars. They stood in the living room window watching the red lights flashing saying, " cool, man, cool". Thank God, the cops didn't come in. My girlfriend told them that I was having a birthday party. They told her to ask me to turn down the music, and that was it! The party picked up its tempo once again, but the music was quieter. My girlfriend Sandy stopped by and asked me what was going on. I told her it was a keg party because she wouldn't approve of the drugs. She gave me the fishy eye, and went home. Later it seemed to me that the party was out of hand, so I went upstairs, grabbed my kids out of bed, and went across the street to Sandy's house to sleep. The next day I went home. What a mess! There was beer spilled everywhere, and holes burned into my carpet. Someone had even pissed on the floor! Someone else had tried to cook, and scorched my pots and pans. I said, "never again". I had to open all the windows and scrub the hell out of the place. It was horrible! Two days later I heard what a great party it was, and that I should have another one. I told them, no way, and I never did.

One night I went out with two of my girlfriends. We went to my favorite Indian bar and played Foosball, and listened to the jukebox. This gorgeous hunk of Indian came over and offered to buy me a drink. I said no, because I didn't want to be bothered at that time. When we were leaving he asked me if he could come with us, I said no, and told him that I would catch him later. Well, a week later I caught him. I was at the same bar with my girlfriends, and he approached me with a drink. I took it, and he sat down with us. His name is Darren. We ended up bar hopping with him in tow. He was a Marine, fresh out of Vietnam, with a lot of mental baggage, and at the time, I didn't have a clue. He drank too much, but I didn't think anything of it. I considered it, too much partying. I saw him on and off. We had not yet become an item. I was seeing his uncle every now and then, when he would come into town. I was playing the field big time, and having a ball.

To give you a glimpse of the magnitude of Darren's problem, I have to tell you about a New Years Eve party that we went to. It was at a nice club, and *there were a lot of people. My sister Kate and her husband were with us at a table, and we were also joined by my ex-husband and wife number three. I liked to dance, but Darren didn't know how, so I tried to teach him. It was like pushing a sandbag around so I stopped trying to dance with him, and took up watching everyone else have a good time. I am also observing Darren. He is drinking straight whiskey from a bottle. I was mortified, but no one was paying attention. When it came time for the buffet, I went up and got us each a plate of food. Dummy that I was, thought that I could sober Darren up by getting him to eat. Every one was sitting around eating and talking. After they ate, they got up to dance. I was sitting watching Darren. All of a sudden, he puked into his plate, and then without missing a drunken beat, tossed the plate under the table and onto the floor! My God! I couldn't believe what was happening! I was thankful that no one else saw him do it. After the party, everyone wanted to go out for breakfast. I just wanted to go home. It was not to be. My ex-husband grabbed us and took us to an eatery. It was so packed that we had to leave. My ex dropped us off home.*

Darren staggered up stairs looking for another party. I went up after him to get him back down into our house, and I couldn't believe my eyes. There were broken bottles and glasses all over, along with busted furniture and cigarette butts on the floor. It looked like there had been a battle royal. I managed to get Darren back down stairs.

He sat at the table mumbling about the war. And still I didn't get the alcohol thing, and by now, I was feeling so bad for this man, and all his pain, that I thought that I could make him better. I was never so wrong about anything in my whole life, as I was about this problem. I couldn't fix it, but I didn't understand why. Little did I know that the road to my hell would be paved by my good intentions.

There was another cute guy from the rez that I was seeing. He and I would sit on the hood of my car, eat sardines and crackers, and wash it down with beer, while we listened to the tunes on the car radio. This man was a real cutie, and had a great sense of humor, and was as gentle as a baby lamb. Our relationship wasn't so much about sex as it was about fun and laughter. I recall one day when he and I were under the grape arbor in my back yard. It started to rain, and we ended up on the ground just hugging and rolling around getting soaked. I can still see his cigarettes floating by, the rain was coming down so hard, and we were laughing like two kids. He was a lot of fun, but he drank too much too. But he was a happy drunk. I didn't learn about alcoholism until later on. I didn't know or understand it, as being a disease, not yet.

Oh yes, I was still having sex without giving it a thought. It was just a part of the dating scene now. Everyone was doing it. Make love, not war. So, I did. The best part of all this was the fact that I kept my behavior from my two little ones. They never saw a man in my house. When I was having a good time, I made sure they were well taken care of and shielded from my night- life.

Darren kind of slid in to my life real slow and sneaky. I say slow and sneaky because, every time he came over he managed to leave something behind, in the line of clothing. He was the gorgeous hunk of Indian that I caught the night I was out with my girlfriends. He was ten years younger than I, but it didn't bother me because I looked and acted ten years younger than I was. Slowly he moved in, and the next thing I knew, he was a permanent fixture. My little boy Luke didn't like him, and one day when I was putting Luke down for his nap, Darren came in and sat on the foot of my son's bed. Luke proceeded to kick at him, telling him to go home. I hushed Luke and told him to take his nap. Luke was jealous of Darren because in his little boy mind he felt that Darren was taking me away from him I guess. Little Storm was too small to care one way or the other.

I had a car that I had bought real cheap. It was a nice little Blue Ford Falcon. Darren borrowed it one day so that he could go to the rez for whatever. He didn't come back until late that night, and when he did, he was out of breath, because he had run home to tell me that he had hit a parked car, two blocks away from my house. He was drunk. My car was totaled., and I was pissed!

Darren went to school and became a certified welder, and got a job, and bought us another car. It didn't last long because, like a dummy, he towed a buddy of his who had gotten stuck in the snow, and burned out the transmission. I had forewarned him that this might happen, as there was a lot of ice on the ground, but what did I know? I was a only a woman. Darren bought us another car. It was a beautiful white Chevy Camaro convertible. Life really became somewhat normal, except for Darren's drinking. I would get up in the morning, iron his work clothes, fix breakfast and make his lunch, up until the time he was laid off his job. He lost it because he couldn't get up after a night of drinking and go to work. Something had to be done, so I got a job as a meat wrapper to support us. And then the worst thing happened. I got pregnant! And once again I am in the shocked mode. As if it was something new! And on top of it, Darren was sneaking around with another woman! Being a meat wrapper is not as easy as it sounds. Sometimes I had to lift heavy trays of meat to put in the cases. This work, and the stress of Darren's betrayal, and drinking, caused me to have a miscarriage. It was just as well, and I didn't feel anything about it one way or another, and I didn't really want any more kids.

I confronted Darren with the knowledge of his girlfriend, and he dropped her. Once again, I was happy. I thought. I couldn't understand his need to drink, as I had stopped all together. One evening we had an argument. I picked up a baby bottle filled

151

with milk and hit him across the face with it. Well, he in turn, went to hit me with a right hook, but caught me in the back of the neck, causing me to spin like a tipsy ballerina. When I hit the wall, I rebounded and jumped on his back, hanging on with my legs, all the time I'm popping him in the head. He finally shook me off and left the house. He didn't come back for two days. When he did, we never mentioned what had happened between us, and life became rather routine.

One evening the kids were in bed, and Darren and I were watching TV when I saw a shadow out side the front window. I went to see what or who it was, and you'll never guess. It was Craig! I couldn't believe it! He needed a place to hide out from the cops, so he came to me for help. I had to ask Darren if it would be all right. After all, Craig was an ex boyfriend and they knew each other. Darren said OK. I asked Craig what happened. It seems that he beat the hell out of his new bride, and destroyed his aunt's house in the process. They had a warrant out for his arrest. He went to Benton PA and hid out there for a while, but wanted to come back and check on his wife without being caught. He asked me if I would go up to the hospital to see how she was doing and give her a letter. I did, and I was shocked at what I saw. Her jaws were wired as they had been broken in several places, the whites of her eyes were flaming red, with no white showing at all, and she had to learn how to walk and talk all over again, he had beaten her so bad. I said to myself," there *but for the grace of God, go I". The sad part of all of this was that he really did love her but his mind was twisted from the war, and the beating was the result of his demons. They never got back together and she divorced him and moved to the other end of the country. I came home and told Craig what I had observed, and that I had given her his letter. She read it but gave me no answer. He didn't stay to long after that, however, while he was at my house he saved it from catching on fire. It seems that while I was at work, Darren had fallen asleep, and Luke let a little friend in to play in the cellar. Craig smelled smoke and went downstairs just in time to put the fire out. Luke's little friend had a lighter and was showing it off by setting a piece of paper on fire. Needless to say, Craig sent the boy home, and reprimanded Luke, and all the time, Darren was asleep. And he was supposed to be babysitting! Craig left my house and went back to the rez and worked things out with his aunt.*

And, you will never guess. But yes you have, and you are right. I am pregnant once again however this will be the last time. For real. Darren wanted me to have an abortion, but I said, "no way". I told him that he didn't have to stay because I could take care of myself, and that I didn't need him, I had been through it before by myself. He was not a happy camper, and continued to drink.

Meanwhile, my friend upstairs moved out, and another girl moved in. She was a strip dancer at some chintzy night- club downtown, and she had a mouth on her like you couldn't imagine. The worst word I ever used was shit or ass. Her every sentence was filled with words like, fuck, fucker, cunt, or cock-sucker. I was shocked! And she had two little boys under four years old. She would have a different guy upstairs every night. Darren and I could hear the bed bumping all the way down in to our living room. We would time the action. And I could tell that the guy never even washed up afterwards, because the sound of the footsteps went from the bed and down the stairs. Yuk! I guess this was how she supplemented her income. I didn't care. It was her life. However, she was always pissing me off. She wouldn't watch her kids, and they would get up early in the morning and throw their tricycles down the back stairs, which were right next to my bedroom. They would also shit in the hall by my back door. One day they got up real early and got into my car, where they found a watermelon. They managed to break it open and eat it in my car. They also took the door locks off.. They had made one hell of a mess. They also took some of that watermelon and dragged it over to the next- door neighbor's porch and made another mess there. I yelled upstairs and told that girl she had better get up and take care of her kids. Every one was pissed.

During one hot July day, Darren and I took the kids to the beach and stayed until it got dark. We pulled into the driveway. When we got out of the car, we noticed that the side of the house looked kind of white, and wavy. Upon closer examination we found the whiteness to be millions of maggots! They were everywhere! It seems that the girl upstairs did not cover her garbage as usual, and this was the result. Darren went down stairs into the cellar and got the hose. He hooked it up to the hot water tank and washed the side of the house down where the maggots were. You would have had to see it to believe it. The next day the birds came and ate all the dead things up. I called the landlord and bitched. He said he would talk to her. Things were quiet for a while.

Darren is still drinking, and I am getting fatter in my pregnancy. When he is sober, he doesn't want to know anything about the baby, but when he is hung over he would caress my stomach to feel it kick. He wanted a girl. This was the softer side of him, and I only saw it when he was hung over. He was totally different. The drinking is getting worse, and seems to be more often. Darren leaves and doesn't come home sometimes. He spends his time on the reservation, with his friends drinking and whoring around. Once in awhile his brother Chris would come by for a visit, and then they would both drink, and get drunk. The only difference is that his brother would get mean when he was drunk. One time I tried to open my mouth to object to something when Chris slammed his fist down on the table and told me, 'this is men's talk, and none of your business". That scared the shit out of me, so I kept my mouth shut and tried to make sure Chris didn't come over very often.

Chris did end up having to stay with us much to my chagrin. It wasn't too bad because he couldn't drink. He had been hit by a Volkswagen. It was a hit and run. Everybody was making a joke out of the accident because the VW drove off in a shambles because Chris was so big. He was 6 feet six inches tall. The reason he ended up staying with us was because he had a broken leg, and there was no indoor plumbing at the house on the rez. He needed to be able to get to a toilet without having to use stairs.

At this time, we had little or no food at all. And these two guys were big eaters. I would manage to make a huge pot of pork soup now and then Chris would yell from the bedroom that he wanted more, but Darren would just yell back, "ration, ration"! When I look back I can laugh about it now, but I couldn't then.

It was a very bad time in my life. It was called welfare and it sucked. While Chris and Darren were home they would watch the kids while I would walk to the store. One evening I went to the store. When I came back the kids were in bed. I went in to check on them. Luke was asleep. I walked over to Storms crib and noticed that he was covered right up to his chin, and he was looking at me with frightened eyes. Something was wrong. I pulled back his blankets to discover that Chris and Darren had tied Storm's *little hands and feet to the crib! I was so pissed off! I untied, comforted him, and laid him back down, and then I went into the living room and went on the warpath. I raised holy hell, and threw Chris out of the house. They said that they didn't mean any harm. They thought it was funny. And the sad thing about it, it was true. They didn't know any better. That was how they were raised. These brothers have a very twisted sense of humor.*

Darren, the boy's, and I were all asleep one night when pounding on the kitchen door awakened me. I stumbled out of bed, and went to the door to see who it was. I pulled the curtains back to see the girl upstairs standing there, crying with a black and blue face. I opened the door to let her in, and found out what the problem was. It seemed that her boyfriend came home and beat her up because she forgot to remove her makeup before he got home. He didn't allow her to wear it so when he wasn't around, she would. Funny thing, he was Indian too. These guys could give Indian People a bad rep.

One summer evening I had been sitting outside chatting with my next- door neighbor. I decided to go in the house to get a drink. As I walked into the dining room, I saw a roach skitter across the wall. I was furious! I knew exactly where it came from, upstairs. I called my neighbor's son-in-law to come in and kill it, and take it out. After he removed it, I proceeded to take all the food out of my cupboards and throw away what was opened, and put the rest into the fridge. And then I scrubbed the cupboards. I couldn't stand the thought that a roach may have been in my food. Yuk! The thought even makes me gag today. The next day I called my landlord and told him what had happened. He wasn't upset at all. He told me to buy some roach killer and spray around the bathroom sink, which he figured was where they were coming in from. I did, and I kept watch to make sure that they didn't make it to the rest of my house.

Life at this time was hell on earth. I was surrounded by drunks. Upstairs, next door, and in my own home. It seemed that Darren was drunk all the time. He wasn't a mean drunk unless he drank whiskey, and then he was hell on wheels. When he drank beer he would just be stupid sounding, and he would sit at the table and mumble about being a Marine and the war. It was so disgusting. My boys were usually asleep so they didn't get to hear his crap, not until they got older.

Here is a poem that I had written about the drinking, and how I felt about it at the time. I called it Semper Fi.

SEMPER FI
I hate drinking,
And stinking thinking.
Sleepless nights,
 and drunken fights.

Empty tears,
And pride profane,
killing off a sodden brain.
Yelling, screaming, nasty mean,
Look at me, I'M A MARINE!

Dress Blues and Olive Drab,
Soon they'll lay him on a slab,
Just another broken soul,
Who was looking to be whole.

He drank the white man's great whiskey,
And lived for his next beer,
I sit and wonder,
And as I watch...
My heart is filled with fear.
The question races through my mind,
will he be here next year?

Darren had a multitude of problems that stemmed from his childhood, and his time in Vietnam. When he was around fourteen, his mother shot and killed his father. His father was abusive, and would come home drunk and beat the hell out of his mother. I guess she had enough, so one night he started in on her, and she grabbed a loaded rifle and let him have it. She was pregnant, and later died from complications after childbirth. A year or two later, their house burned. There were ten children all together. The grandmother, with the help of the older brother took care of them. In our first year together, he had an uncle that was killed while

159

he was working on iron, and then, his grandfather committed suicide. I wasn't used to this aspect of life, and I felt very bad for Darren. I thought that if I loved him enough, and tried to understand him, that I could take away his pain, and make everything all better. Yeah...right. "Dumb as a box of rocks or what?" I had no clue about the disease of alcoholism, and wouldn't learn until many years later.

One incident that sticks in my mind and shaped my way of handling my feelings was that one night I had been sitting on the pity pot and I started to cry. Darren heard me and said, "stop that crying." I don't like it, and it won't get you anywhere". The funny thing is, that I did stop, and my grandmother's words came ringing back in my head about tears not getting me anywhere, so after that I became somewhat of a hard ass, and would never cry where anyone could see, or hear me. I'd be damned before I would let anyone think I was weak or wimpy.

On the evening of September 25th 1973 I started to have labor pains. Darren wasn't home. He had gone out to the rez, so the next day I got a sitter for Luke and Storm and I started to walk to the rez. I figured that Darren might be coming home and I could run into him on his way back. It would have been a nine mile walk. The pains were close but not too hard, so I kept on walking. I had walked about two miles, and then it started to sprinkle, so I turned around and headed back home before it poured. I called my girlfriend that lived across the *street and she came over and stayed with me until my labor became unbearable. Meanwhile Darren showed up hung over, with a black eye and a chipped front tooth. He had been in a drunken brawl. My friend and I took the boys to her house and left them with her older daughter and son, and then she took me to the hospital and dropped me off. The delivery was horrible, because it was natural, with nothing for pain, and the baby weighed ten pounds! I didn't scream or anything. I just did what the doctor coached me to do. There were two doctors, and two nurses because I was considered high risk, but it all turned out well, and our daughter, and my last baby, was born. This pregnancy was nine months of hell, but not because of being pregnant, but because of the hellish crap I went through with all the drunks.*

Darren was so proud of the baby that he brought one of his uncles up to see her, and they both held her, of course, they were both half in the bag. We named her Michelle. I had made up my mind to be sterilized, as I never wanted to go through nine more months of the hell that I had already been through. Can you imagine? Why in hell did it take so long for the light bulb to go on in my head?

It's hard to explain what it's like living with, and around alcoholics. If I had been passive, maybe it wouldn't have been so bad, but I wasn't. I vented like a locomotive! And when I did, I put myself at risk of being belted, but I knew just how far I could go. And all I ever wanted was a quiet, peaceful, loving and gentle marriage. Now, wasn't that just a laugh? My situation was anything but. Like I said, when Darren was sober, he was terrific. Oh, and I forgot to mention the one thing that was fun about this relationship. The next day, after he had been on a drunk, we had great sex. Out of all the men I had played with, he was the only one that was able to make me climax, and I loved it. That was the flip side of all the bullshit. I look back and try to figure out why I stayed in such a psychologically abusive relationship. I thought I was in love, I knew he needed me, the sex was the greatest, and I also needed any money that he could contribute to our survival. "There are none so wise, as those who have survived stupidity", just ask me.

For someone that didn't want to be a father, he did quite well at it. We took turns with the feeding times in the night. When it was time for Michelle to have her daily bath, he would turn up the heat, and lock the kitchen door so no one would come in and create a draft. He also bathed her. He wouldn't let anyone touch her that didn't wash his or her hands, and he wouldn't let anyone in the house that had a cold. In that respect he was good, but he would still get drunk.

I was in the bedroom changing Michelle's diaper when I saw a cockroach run across the top of the dresser. That was it! They had come back. I called my landlord and told him that I would be moving out as soon as I found another house. As luck would have it, Kate's mother-in-law was moving out of her house and into a trailer, and she wanted to rent the place. It was in the suburbs, and across the street from several acres of woods. It had three bedrooms, a good sized kitchen, small living and dining room, and a great back yard. It also had an attached garage. The only problem with this house is that it was so dirty, and smelled like cat piss. The garage reeked of dog shit. It seems that the owner let her cats do what they wanted where and when they wanted to, and her dog, lived the same way in the garage. The rent was real cheap so I rented it. I cleaned and I painted. Darren had the job of cleaning and deodorizing the garage, which was horrendous. My brother-in-law even came over and washed the windows. When it was finished it was absolutely adorable, and ready for us to move in. Before we moved to our new house, I took every piece of clothing and anything where a roach could possibly hide, and shook it out in the driveway before I packed it. I wanted to make sure that I wasn't going to bring them along with me, and I didn't.

My sister Kate, her husband, and their two boys lived on the street directly behind us. We all got along pretty well. My sister and her husband both worked. Something happened to their baby sitter, so they asked me if I would watch my nephews and they would pay me fifteen dollars a week. I said ok. The oldest boy, David was in Kindergarten. He didn't like the fact that I would make him change *his clothes after school. I also made him pick up after himself, and he didn't like that either, so he complained to his father. His father decided to try and let him stay at home alone after school because I could see their house, and entry doors from my place. Well, one day all hell broke loose! My brother-in-law called me on the phone and had me go to their house. He had something he wanted me to see. I went over. Well, it seemed that someone had gone into their bedroom and thrown stuff all over the place. My brother-in-law asked me if I had seen anyone at the house other than David. I said no, because I didn't. The only one in that house was David. David had gone into their bedroom looking for games that they had, and while he was looking he made a mess. The problem being that he lied, and his father truly believed that he didn't do it, until he decided to call the police. Then David confessed, because he was afraid of the police coming to his house. At first my brother-in-law inferred that maybe one of my boys came in the house and did it. There was no way, because I wouldn't even let my kid's onto their property when they weren't home, for this reason. If anything happened, I wouldn't want them to get the blame.*

My sister's kid's were spoiled and had every toy imaginable. I think that was their way of making up to their kids because they worked. They were volunteers, and were away from home a lot, especially the father. David had an electric car, and they had a train that they could actually ride around in their front yard. I remember that on Fridays that they would always take their kids out to eat dinner. David was a pretty good kid, but his younger brother Troy had behavioral problems. I recall being at their house one Saturday morning. David was watching cartoons and very content. Troy was bugging David to play with him. David kept ignoring Troy. Pretty soon their father went into the living room and physically forced David to go outside and play with his little brother. I was pissed, but I kept my mouth shut as usual. What I saw and heard was not fair to David. Troy was a real brat.

Michelle had her first birthday in this house, and her brothers adored her and usually gave her whatever they had, that she might want. I also had my first major surgery while living there. Darren's grandmother came and took care of the kids while I was in the hospital. She was a real sweetheart and loved all of them.

I was in the hospital when Darren's birthday came. The grandmother made him an apple pie. When she went to put it in the oven, she couldn't get it to work, so she ended up taking it to her house to bake. I thought that was sweet of her to do. I was in the hospital for two weeks. When I came home, Darren was very helpful. He would clean my incision, and dress it. He also waited on me. This was also the only Christmas that he had ever bought me presents. I will never forget it. He gave me a real gold cross with a diamond in it, and matching earrings. He also gave me a beautiful Hunter Green Velour Robe, by Vanity Fair, slippers, and a nightgown. I always told him it was because he was afraid that I might die during my surgery, and he wanted a clear conscience.

In our twenty-eight years together, he had never bought me another Christmas gift. In fact, that was the first and last time I had ever received any type of gift from him. I, however, always tried to give him what he wanted or needed, just as I did with the kids. I thought that after so many years it would sink in, that Christmas was about giving and making people happy. This was always, and still is, my favorite time of the year. (except for the time that I was on leave from reform school) I guess that when he was a child, this was the worst time of the year for him, this, and autumn hold bad memories. There was never a Christmas Eve that he didn't get plastered, but as usual I would keep it together, and forget about New Year's Eve. We never went to another party after the one where he threw up in his dinner. I would just stay home, and he would go out alone, or with one of the guys from work.

Darren is now an ironworker, and still drinking like a thirsty fish. One Friday he never came home from work and no one on the rez had seen him. I ended up calling the State Police because I thought something horrible had happened to him. The State Police were very nice. They even asked me if I had enough groceries in the house, and of course I did. Late the second night Darren came home. He told me that he *had gone out drinking with a bunch of Mohawks after work. He had gotten drunk, so they put him in the back of their pickup and went up north to Canada, and took him with them. Whenever he would drink he never gave the consequences a thought, and he never gave us a thought either. This was all part of the disease and I still didn't have a clue. I just thought that he was being irresponsible. The "box of rocks" was dumber than ever.*

I only lived behind my sister for a year, and after all that scrubbing and painting. Her mother-in-law didn't like living in a trailer, so she wanted to move back into her house, so I had to find another place to live. I had a two-year lease and could have stayed if I wanted to push it, but why bother. I didn't need or want the hassle. I took pictures of the inside of the house as proof that it was clean and painted when we left, because she was the type of woman that liked to make up gossip, and I didn't trust her. She was a drunk.

I found another little house two blocks over at the top of the hill. It had one large bedroom, but a huge attic that I converted into a bedroom for the boys. It also had a large yard and plenty of room for a dog.

We lived in this house for four years. The boys made friends and were able to walk to school. They joined Cub Scouts and took part in sports. I became an assistant Den Mother. I also became an Emergency

Medical Technician and joined our local ambulance corps as a driver. Everything was normal except for the drinking, and little did I know that our life wasn't normal at all. We were what would become to be known as, a dysfunctional family. You could have fooled me. Sometimes I think that all of this is a bunch of crap. If we were dysfunctional, then so are the majority of the people on this planet. It all depends on who is calling whom what, and by what standards they are using to make the judgment. No one is perfect, and no one will ever achieve the kind of perfection that will allow him or her to be totally functional. What is good for one, is not necessarily good for the other, but these are just my opinions.

Darren had settled into his life pretty well but was still drinking. In the summer we would rent a small motor boat and take the kids out to the lake. In the winter, Darren would go outside and build snowmen with them or take them sled riding down the reservoir hill. He would even take them Halloweening while I stayed at home to hand out candy. In all respects I thought that he was a pretty good father, and stepfather, except for the drinking. But how would I know what a father was supposed to do? I didn't have one when I was their age. The sad part of this whole story is that the kids don't remember much of the good times, only the bad. They were now getting older and were able to see and hear him first hand, and they didn't like it.

Darren had a younger brother. All the family adored Theadore. He was like a clown always running, playing jokes and laughing. Theadore also drank but didn't get drunk. He would come and stay with us once in awhile and it was like having another kid in the house except he was eighteen. He was a good boy, but I always bitched Darren out about giving Teddy beer to drink. The bitching fell on deaf ears.

One day we received a phone call That Teddy was hit by a car and in the hospital. We were both under the impression that Teddy only had a broken leg and would be all right. We went to the hospital only to find out that both of his legs had been severed. The doctors did a great job of re-attaching them, and the surgery was working. Darren and I went in to see him. We made small talk and told him to hang in there, and that we would see him tomorrow. Something went wrong and they shipped him to a different hospital. He died there. I think he willed it, because he thought that he would be in a wheelchair for the rest of his life and he wouldn't be able to live with that. This was a horrible time for the whole family. Darren handled it by drinking worse than ever. One night he was curled up howling like a wounded animal. I wanted to take the rifle and put him out of his misery. I came so close. I had never heard such wailing from a human being in my life.

Darren would still disappear to the rez and drink, and he was still whoring around. He had wrecked our Chevy Malibu when he was on one of his drunks, and we had to get another vehicle. After one of his nights out, he came home rather early. I took the car and went to the store. I put the bags of groceries in the car and didn't pay any attention to what was in the back seat. When I got home, I was taking the bags out, when I looked down, and there, sticking out from under the car seat was a stinking dirty sanitary napkin! I ripped off a part of the bag and used it to grab the stinking thing. I then went raging into the house with it in my hand screaming at him about screwing around on me. When Darren heard me, he grabbed Michelle and ran upstairs to the boy's room. He used her as a shield, because I think he felt that I was going to kill him for sure, and I was so angry and humiliated that I could have. I wanted to kill him with a good heart. Of course he denied it, saying that it was from his buddy's girlfriend, and that they were in the back seat while he was driving around. Yeah, right, and I was Cleopatra.

Our new car didn't last very long because Darren crashed it into a ditch on the rez. His sister brought him home. By now I was getting tired of all this crap and drunkeness that I was getting to the point where I didn't want him around. I told his sister that I didn't want him in my house, and I asked her why she brought him to my home. She said it was because he didn't have any place else to go. I discovered that Darren was cheating on me with another female. I have to refer to her as that because she was *a fifteen year old slut, who was already pregnant by someone else. Her mother knew how she was, and let her get away with it. I wasn't about to. I tracked her and her mother down. Through several pretexts I was able to get their phone number and address. I found out that the girl's mother was a barmaid. I went to her workplace and confronted her about her daughter, and what her daughter was doing with my boyfriend. She thought that I was mistaken. We agreed to meet in a public place the next day so that I could fill her in on her daughter's behavior. We met and I told her everything. The mother said that her daughter was engaged to be married. She was shocked to know that her daughter was pregnant. I had this all figured out. The whole damned family was white trash. The mother let young runaways stay at her house, and they in turn would have parties while dear old mom worked. After I put an end to this affair, I asked Darren why he cheated on me. Are you ready for this? He said it was because I didn't run around the house in little see through nighties! I asked him if he was nuts. We had three kids. There was no more cheating after this episode. (not that I knew of).*

We had now been together for six years. Pretty soon, I would be considered Darren's common law wife. There was no way I wanted to be a common anything so I gave him a choice. Get married, or get out. He chose to get married. In a small civil ceremony with his brother and sister-in-law as our witnesses, we were married. It was no big deal, but it was better than being a common law wife. He did buy me a diamond engagement ring and we had matching wedding bands, however, he never wore his, and it was later stolen.

After four years of living in the house we decided to move into an apartment complex with a swimming pool. We were movin on up. Darren and I both had good paying blue-collar jobs, and we could afford the move. Now each of the kids had bedrooms. The boys shared a very large bedroom, and Michelle had a normal sized one, and ours was huge. For the first time in years there was more than enough food, and for the first time in my life I could pick up a piece of meat and not look at the price. We had credit cards and charge accounts, all being paid on time. Our credit was excellent. Darren still drank as much as ever, but managed to hold his job for five years. I went from working in a factory to becoming a Security Guard for an aluminum company. This position called for me to work the third shift, and Darren hated it. He was working second shift, so we never got to see each other until weekends. One night I received a phone call at work. Michelle called me to tell me that Darren was drunk and that he was being mean. I called my partner and told him that my daughter had an earache and that my husband couldn't find the ear- drops, so I would have to leave. He said that he would cover for me while I went home to take care of it. When I arrived home Darren was falling down drunk. He had been in the whiskey, and that was bad news. He caught Luke trying to sneak out the bedroom window and beat him with a belt. He also rampaged in the boy's room and threw their mattresses off the bed and tore things up. He was a maniac. I managed to get him into the living room where I tried to talk some sense into him. He wouldn't listen and became belligerent. By now I had had it with his bullshit. I took a flying leap across my glass coffee table and tackled him, knocking him to the couch, with me on top of him. I put my hands around his throat and squeezed to get his attention. He kept insisting that I let him up, and I insisted that he knock off his crap and leave the kids alone. He finally agreed, and I let him up. (Interesting that something got through to his brain). He went outside and was sitting on the steps. This would not have been a bad thing, except that it was snowing and cold. I was worried that he would freeze to death. I tried to get him back in to the apartment, but he wouldn't come in. I called the police. They knew him and liked him. They came and managed to get him into the apartment, whereupon he passed out. I sent the kids back to bed and assured them that he wouldn't bother them, and then I went back to work. I did tell them that if there was another problem to call me at work. The rest of the night was quiet.

We lived there for three years. We both had our own motorcycles and would go riding with my sister who also had a bike. We would take the kids camping at the lake on my two weeks vacation or we would rent a motor boat and pack a picnic lunch and take the kids on the river and lake. Life was good except for the drinking.

Drugs were starting to make their way into the complex, and I wanted to get my kids away from there. I also wanted to give them some stability and keep them in the same school until they graduated, so I started to look for a house that we could afford to buy. We found one, right in back of my sisters, and we bought it. It was small and looked like a hunting lodge with three bedrooms. I fell in love with it. There were woods across the street and an empty lot next door on the corner. It was almost like living in the country. The owner said that the woods would always be there, and that no one could build on the lot next door, and like a dummy, I believed him. Of course, me not being pushy or nosey, also failed to look around really good, and we were screwed. After the old owners moved out, we could then see all the things that were wrong with it. Putty was falling from the windowpanes, paint was coming off the sills, and they ripped up the wall-to-wall carpeting, and there was a big hump in the living room floor. We didn't notice it with the carpeting. One nice thing was that all the floors were a natural hardwood and in good condition. However, I wanted wall-to-wall carpeting to help keep the house warm in the winter, and keep the noise down when you walked so I covered them up again. We had a fireplace in the living room and a small pot bellied stove in the kitchen. It was very cozy. From then on all the family Christmas get togethers were at our *house. They were great parties except that Darren always managed to get plastered, and when every one went home, he would turn into a real jerk. As a matter of fact, he did this at all holiday functions. Not a holiday ever went by that he didn't get drunk and ruin it.*

I still did not have a clue about alcohol being a disease, and was frustrated by his lack of control. One summer eve he was drunk and thought he was going to manhandle me and slap me around. I took care of that and hit him twice in the legs with a baseball bat. The next day he asked me to take a look at his bruised legs, and said, "look what you did to me." I told him why he had the bruises, and also told him that worse things would happen to him if he ever tried to hit me again. He never tried to hurt me after that. It's too bad, now that I think of it. If he had ever actually beaten me up, he would never been allowed to stay in my life, and I would have never subjected my children, and myself to his drunken tirades. Go figure, however, I never thought about all the emotional, and mental abuse that I was living with. I didn't have a clue.

After our second year in the house Darren decided to go out to the rez and go hunting. He was up in a tree (raking leaves, no, just kidding) and lost his footing when he spotted a deer. In his excitement he forgot where he was, and took the wrong step. He fell out of the tree and broke his back. He was alone, but new if he didn't get out of the woods he would die before anyone found him, so he crawled to a road, and was found and taken to the hospital. He collected disability and I continued to work and take care of him.

There was a time during his recovery from his broken back that he decided to go to work and see all the guys. The only problem was, that he went there drunk. His foreman saw him reach into his pocket, and thought he was pulling out a gun and proceeded to call the local police. Come to find out, what he was pulling out of his pocket was a bottle of whiskey. The police brought him home. I didn't want him all drunk and stupid, so they called the local ambulance and had him taken to The Veteran's Hospital, after I told them that he had just been recuperating from a broken back. This would give me a break and some peace and quiet for a while. He was in the hospital for two days and then they let him come home. He wasn't able to go back to that type of work so he had to find something else to do. Meanwhile his drinking picked up.

One day Darren woke up complaining of pains in his stomach. I told him it was probably gas and it would go away. I took him to the VA hospital so they could check him out. They found nothing wrong with him and sent him home. Two days later I rushed him to the hospital with severe stomach pains again. This time it was a ruptured appendix and they had to do an emergency appendectomy. There I was again, making hospital visits, and I still had to work and take care of my kids. When he returned home I had to wash and cleanse the incision and then cover it with a bandage. It took forever to heal because he is a diabetic.

It was months before he went back to work. Meanwhile I was getting behind in our bills. So that I could make the mortgage, I went to Consumer Credit Counseling with all my bills. They helped me and suggested that I go to Albany to see if HUD would take over my mortgage. That way they could put me on a sliding scale and I wouldn't lose the house, and I could still hang on and cope. This all worked out well, and things were going along smoothly.

Darren found a different job that sent him out of town to work. He didn't like it, but the money was good. Once he was sent to Boston, and one weekend I drove down to spend some time with him. Luke was now old enough to baby-sit, so I left him in charge of Michelle, and Storm. While at Darren's hotel room I snooped around and found a bottle of Vodka in his dresser drawer. I just gave him a dirty look.
We went to Cape Cod and then up to the point where the fishing trawlers came in with their catch of the day. We walked along the beach like a couple of people in a romance novel, except that this was no romance, and it was real.

It was December, and it was cold, but it was nice because there were no crowds of people to deal with. We had lunch at a quaint restaurant called

The Snow Goose. It was a pleasant trip, and then it was over. I had to drive back home to reality. This job didn't last long either, as Darren didn't like being away from home, however, he found another one.

I was laid off my job and found another one that was temporary. One day I decided to take his station wagon to work, and I left the truck home because I had to pick up riders. When I returned home after my shift I got a phone call that there had been a terrible accident and someone had been killed. I was like, oh my God! I called my girlfriend, and she came back to my house to baby-sit so I could get up to the hospital and find out what had happened. When I walked into that hospital room and saw Darren, my legs turned to rubber, and I thought I was going to faint. I thought for sure he was going to die. His face was a mess. It was swollen and black and blue, and his nose was barely there. One of his legs was all bandaged up. He was mumbling about who was in the truck with him. He couldn't remember. I didn't know until later the next day that the person that was killed was his uncle. This was one of the most hellish nightmares of my life. There would be two more. All of his cousins wanted him to go to jail, but one of them talked the rest of them out of it. Even though he was drunk, so were the people in the other car, and there was a question of who had hit whom, and it was on the rez. And his cousin felt that Darren was at least good enough to go and take his uncle out drinking, and no one forced him to drink, or get in the ill fated truck. That was the end of that. However, that was a felony DWI. They took his license away for one year, and gave him five years probation. It was wonderful. He couldn't drink or he would get violated and go to jail. Well, let me put it this way, he wasn't supposed to drink but did. He just was very, very careful not to get caught. His Probation Officer was a woman and very nice. As a part of her job she had to make home visits. Whenever she would come she would say how wonderful it was that Darren wasn't drinking and that his life must be getting on track. I wanted so badly to tell her of his hypocrisy. One night he got so plastered that he threw spaghetti all over the kitchen wall. I was so pissed and crying because I couldn't put an end to this madness. The next morning I went to work and called his PO. I told her to take her blue box and go to the house. She would still find him drunk. She did, and she violated him. That night the Sheriff's came, cuffed him and took him away. The judge sent him to a rehabilitation program up in Smokey Lake. I was to drive him there. This was not good because this program wanted the family to take part in his rehabilitation. I dropped him off and was almost killed coming down the mountains after dark. I had hit some black ice and was sliding around. I didn't think I was going to make it back home, but I did.

I had to go to my husband's sister's to see how many wanted to participate in this program. Two out of four said yes. None of the brothers wanted anything to do with it. However, his older brother rented us a car to use while we were up there. The program took care of our housing. This program was horrible, on both the addict and the family. They would put the addict in the hot seat in front of all the other clients, and then each member of the family had to tell him about things that he had done that either hurt, or humiliated them in some way. I wanted no part of this. I went into the ladies room and locked the door. One of the counselors came to get me. I told her that I couldn't do this. She insisted that I had to, and that I could. I told her that I would rather go to a funeral (which I absolutely hated to do). I had no clue that when I said what I did, that I would be going to a funeral a few weeks later. The counselor talked me out of the bathroom and I went into the circle. My husband was in the hot seat.

Our daughter went first, but didn't have too much to say. Luke went second and said nothing, and then... Storm. He spilled his guts about the things that he saw when Darren was drunk. Darren actually had tears in his eyes, but would not let them escape. Only one sister talked, the older one stood by the window crying. And then it was my turn to give him hell for what he put me through. I knew exactly what he was going to say, because he knew it would hurt me to the core, but I was ready. He said, "I don't love you". I said," I know". At that time he hated me for turning him in, or dropping a dime, as he called it. The counselors were flabbergasted. The other men in the group were yelling at him for being so disrespectful, and yelling at him that he should be grateful for having someone like me standing by him.

I held my ground and didn't flinch. The counselors wanted me to cry, and were telling me how much he must have hurt me when he said what he did. But I wouldn't give any of them that satisfaction. Besides, I knew why he said it. He wanted to get even, however, when I look back and think about it, he didn't really love me, I was someone he needed. Someone to take care of him, someone as "dumb as a box of rocks."

Everyday for one week we all had to attend classes on alcoholism and it's affect on the drinker, and the people around them. I learned everything there was to know at that time. Night- time was fun, because at the little house where we stayed we were able to unwind and relax. We also talked, and everyone decided that inside, I was just a marshmallow. The program brought us all a little closer as a family. After the week was over, we all went home. I got to drive through a blinding snowstorm, which I absolutely love to do, and we all made it back in one piece. When I left the program I was under the impression that Darren might not be returning home, as they try and send their patients to other cities to start over. This way they are not subjected to their drinking friends and their partying lifestyle. I didn't know what would happen to Darren, as I did not drink anymore and neither did my friends or family. He only had a month left to go, when disaster struck my family.

I was home and back to work for about two weeks when I got a phone call from my ex-husband. He told me that our oldest boy Tommy had been in a bad automobile accident down in Texas. I didn't know what I was going to do. I had no money to fly down there. My co-workers got together and raised over three hundred dollars so that I could fly to Texas and be with my son. The company told me to take all the time that I needed, and that they would hold my job for me. And here they had just given me a week off for my other problem.

This time I was ready. Armed with a bottle of Valium I landed in Dallas. My ex husband met me at the airport with my son's best friend. The story was that Tommy stopped after work with his friends to have a beer and shoot a game of pool. It was a biker bar. My son's buddy said that when he left, Tommy was fine and shooting pool. Not an hour later he got a phone call that there had been an accident. He went to the hospital. Tommy's co-worker and friend had been thrown from the van. Tommy's head went through the windshield and was hanging out the window. Tommy was brain dead. His co-worker couldn't talk and was busted up bad. We couldn't get any details from him. He was going to be flown to London because that was where he lived. When I first saw Tommy lying in the hospital bed, I thought he was just sleeping. He looked perfect except for his black eye, which was quickly fading to yellow. I talked to him as if he could hear me, but in all reality, he couldn't. My ex and I would go up to the hospital every day to see him and try and talk to his friend. On the fourth day we went to see him and when I went to his room, he wasn't there. I went flying to the nurse's station, and asked where he was. She told me he was gone. I asked her, "gone where"? She said that he had died before we got there. I couldn't believe it. I never really expected him to die. Not really. I am glad I had my Valium because it helped me keep myself together, and to keep from crying. That night one of my other sons arrived with his father's van, and we went out and had a few drinks. That was how Tommy would have wanted it.

Tommy's body was flown home and my granddaughter, my ex, my son, Travis and myself drove back home. The funeral arrangements were made by my ex husband and his fourth wife. We had a closed casket with a picture of him on top of it, because we felt that it would be too hard on the rest of the siblings to see him lying there as if he were only asleep. They were all so close, and this was hell on them. I had to call Darren to let him know what had happened. They let him out three days early so he could be with me and lend me support. What a joke. My support was my Valium. However, one night I locked myself in the bathroom and cried myself sick, and then it was over. I excepted the fact that Tommy was dead and would never come back. That was the reality, and I am a realist. I felt that

Darren at the time, used Tommy's death as a reason to get out of rehab early. When I confronted him with my suspicions, he denied it. And I never brought the subject up again. I am not one to beat sleeping dogs.

Life, as I knew it returned to normal. There was a lay off at my place of employment, but Darren soon found another great paying job with a car company, however, he would take beer to work and would drink on his dinner and breaks. This didn't turn into a problem until the evening that he decided to go for a beer on his lunch break. He was driving his motorcycle. Some guy ran a stop sign and slammed into him. He went flying through the air and landed beneath a parked car. His foot had been torn off and was hanging by some skin. His helmet was knocked off by the force of the impact so he also sustained a head injury, and damage to his right shoulder. And once again I am playing nurse, except this time the burden is heavier. I had to change his bandages four times a day, and make sure that the foot didn't become contaminated by anything foreign. The doctor told me that if his foot became infected they would have to amputate it. This whole affair caused me to come down with asthma due to the stress. I ended up having to treat myself three times a day with a nebulizer, and this was done in between bandage changes.

Every time he had a doctor's appointment I would have to get the wheelchair out, help him into it, wheel him to the car, help him into the car, fold up the chair and put it into the trunk. And then I would repeat the same pattern when we got to the doctor's office. Thank God I was on lay-off when this took place, otherwise I don't know what I would have done. I still had a house and kid's to take care of along with everything else. In the end, his doctor told Darren that he should get down and kiss my feet, because it was really me that had saved his foot. Yeah, right.

Darren never really went back to work after this accident, and his drinking became worse. He spent most of his time on the pity pot, and life really becomes hellish once again. I wrote this poem that pretty much sums up my life with Darren at this point in my life.

The Evil Thing

*When I met him, he was young and handsome,
And he took my heart away
Little did I know
That I would rue the day*

And an evil thing was present...

*I didn't know the evil thing,
Had turned his heart to stone,
and though we were together,
I was still alone*

And the evil thing was gnawing at his spirit...

So, we became a family
And I felt that this was good,
And I became the good wife,
Exactly as I should.

And the evil thing became a part of the family...

Now and then he would break away
From the blackness of the thing,
But always went back to the evil,
And the comfort it would bring.

And the power of the evil thing grew stronger
everyday...

The years were passing one by one,
And all he did was play,
The young man and the evil thing,
Laughing along the way.

And the evil thing was consuming his soul...

The young man grew older,
Always living in the past,
And I stood by him waiting,
How much longer will this last?

And as always, the evil thing is still with us...

Now the evil thing has taken,

The man down to his knees,
But the man cannot see,
The forest, for the trees.

The man is breaking away... he thinks...

So the man feels he has changed,
And better days lie ahead,
Little can he deal with,
The confusion in his head.

And the evil thing has changed it's form,
And found another way,
To keep the man in darkness,,
To keep the love away.

The evil force is all consuming...

The man now thinks he has found the light,
And feels he is getting well,
When all the while the evil thing,
Is taking him to hell...

I returned to work. The work was very physical and I loved it. I would have to lift fifty-pound bags of powder and dump them into a hopper. Sometimes I would have to carry the bags up a ladder to dump them. I was a machine operator and it was a part of my job, along with other physical duties. The temperature in the summer would get up over a hundred and twenty or more around the machines, but I still loved my work. And then I sustained an injury to my back. I stayed out for two days and then went back on light duty. I had to go back because I had no choice. I had to work. After a few months there was going to be another lay off. It was voluntary, so I took it. I felt that if I didn't work for a while that maybe my back would get better. The lay off lasted about three months and my back was feeling pretty good. I was called back, and I was happy. My boss decided to put me on a high-speed assembly line. It was somewhat automated in as much as the line actually moved. I just had to feed it as fast as I could. It was so fast that I was having a hard time getting the parts in the receptacle as they were moving along. At one point I was reaching so far down the line that something happened to my back. All of a sudden I was slammed with excruciating pain, and could barely move. I went to my foreman and told him what had happened. He asked me if I could wait until dinnertime before I left. I told him that I couldn't. I left and went right home. The pain was so intense that I didn't remember the drive home. The next day I went to the doctor's. This was the beginning of a new brand of hell.

You may find this part of my book very boring, but it needs to be told, and someone may benefit from my experience. Before I go into that part of the story I want to say that, men and women are different. Women that do the work of a man will inevitably end up hurting themselves physically. It seems as though most of the women that I know that have worked like men always end up getting hurt. It has been my observation that women who have never worked at physical labor don't get hurt. And Heaven help the woman that do!

This is the voice of experience talking. I know exactly what happens when someone is injured on the job. First, you report the injury, and then you go to the doctor. Meanwhile you get disability, and then the fight really begins. And when it is your back that is hurt, that is even worse. Back injuries are the hardest to pinpoint unless it is something that can be seen on an M.R.I. or a C.A.T. scan. These injuries are known as wounds without scars.

Your doctor may say that you have a problem, but then you are sent to the compensation doctor. He will say that there is little or nothing wrong with you, and all the time you are being treated like some low life piece of crap that is lying. You then get bounced back and forth until the compensation board decides whether you have an injury based on the findings. They will then determine the degree of disability that you have. All the while you are being bounced back and forth your comp. Checks are interrupted, stopped, or sent in an untimely fashion. In some instances marriages break up, and some people have to file bankruptcy. I have also noticed that if you are a comp. patient, the comp. doctor doesn't treat you as well as he would, if you had real insurance, or if you paid cash. As an example, I had an M.R.I. done of my back. The doctor that read the film said that all I had was a lot of arthritis, then one day I went to a chiropractor because I was having debilitating pain, and could barely walk. I had brought my M.R.I. films with me. She took the films to a spine doctor and had him read them. Well, he actually found a problem. That was because, based on my complaints, he had an idea what to look for. Also, he didn't know I was a comp. patient. What does this tell you? You don't have to be a rocket scientist to figure it out. The injured worker is put through bureaucratic hell, and no one gives a damn. My best advice is; if you get injured on the job, beg, or borrow the money and go to a good doctor. Pay for it yourself. That way you will really know what the problem is, and then get a really good attorney. You're going to need one.

For the past ten years I have been out of the work force. Not because I wanted to be out of work, but because my pain kept me out. I couldn't, and still cannot walk, bend, sit, or stand for long periods of time without it causing a great deal of pain. The original back injury has resulted in arthritis of my spine, and pinched nerves. I also have three bad vertebrae in my neck, which also causes problems. My chiropractor discovered this when she had x-rays taken to see why I was having shoulder, and neck problems. I am sure this was caused by my work also, but because it wasn't a complaint at the time of my back injury, it is not covered by comp.

And now, back to the boxing ring of life. In the past ten years I have been in and out of the emergency room for a heart problem, kidney stones, asthma, panic attacks and severe vertigo. And all of these problems were caused by stress. Between the back problems and the stress, I practically live on pain meds, and Xanax. If I do nothing physical, then I have no pain, but life demands that you get up and move, and with my life, I have no other choice.

At some point during all these problems, Darren was pulled over by a sheriff for driving while intoxicated. He ended up going into a rehab program and was put on probation once again, and once again, lost his driver's license. While he was there I never got to speak to him. He went from that program into a halfway house. I tried several times to call him, but he wouldn't talk to me. I had to know what was going on, so I managed to get the name of his counselor, and I called him to find out. The counselor was a real jerk. He called me a controlling woman. I told him that I was left holding the financial bag, and that I had no utilities, as they had been turned off, and I needed to know what Darren was going to do, as I felt he had a certain degree of responsibility towards me. Well, this guy raised his voice at me, and told me that Darren didn't owe me anything, and that he, didn't give a fuck about me. (He really used that word). He told me that he was only concerned about Darren. He also told me that Darren was starting a whole new life without me, and that I had better accept it. There was no way that I was going to let this go, as I was hopping mad! I called my son Storm and told him what had transpired. He was so angry that he went to the halfway house to find this guy and give him a piece of his mind as he felt the counselor was very unethical in his treatment of me. Needless to say, he didn't find the guy and was escorted out of the establishment.

I knew that eventually I would find out where Darren went, because he would want to talk to our daughter and see our granddaughter at some point in time. I went out and bought a caller I.D. and attached it to our daughter's phone. Before I knew it, he called, and up popped his new phone number. It was only a matter of time before I tracked him down to his new home. He had moved into a cute little house in the country, and was sharing it with another guy. The other guy was an American Indian also, and a skirt chaser. He also fancied himself as a Medicine Man of sorts. However, it was more like magic, than medicine. My husband became his willing student and fell for all his mumbo jumbo, and he helped Darren put together what I call a "mojo" bag, but they called it a medicine bag, that is supposed to draw women to you. He was teaching him how to attract women. Together, they would go to their AA meetings, and try to pick up women. They weren't practicing the twelve steps, but the thirteenth step. They were also using marijuana for maintenance because they couldn't drink.

The relationship between these two was really bizarre. My husband was weak minded, and his buddy took advantage of it. This relationship propelled me *into writing the following controversial poem. You must understand. This poem does not apply to all American Indians in recovery programs, but to a very small group that my husband was hanging out with at this particular time. Here it is.*

THE BLACK HORSE

They ride The Black Horse,
of smoke and snow, these Warriors, once so brave,
And they don't even give a damn,
If it puts them in the grave.

So the fallen Warriors gather,
And grumble about the war,
And speak of their tortured spirits,
While searching for a whore.

And The Black Horse beckons....

They sit around and meditate,
To the sounds of flutes and drums,
But little do they know,
That something wicked comes

And The Black Horse is looking for a rider....

These Braves, they have no feelings,
For gentleness or love,
They wander and they wait,
For a sign from up above
Lo! The Thunder Beings will come,

And make them men once more,
To heal their mind and bodies,
And let their spirits soar.

But, The Black Horse gives them power now,
And keeps them from their pain,
But when the ride is over,
There is darkness, once again.

So they run around in circles,
And hang their heads in shame,
And look around to see,
Where they can place the blame.

And The Black Horse is waiting....

They think they're fooling everyone,
But little do they know,
That where The Black Horse takes them,
A sane one would not go.

So the Warrior sits, in his cloud of smoke,
And sheds an empty tear,
Then climbs upon The Black Horse,
To ride away his fear.

Darren was running an ad in one of our local rags. It was in the section where you look for men and women to go out with. I guess he snagged a few dates, but they didn't work out. I managed to talk to one of these women, and she told me that Darren was actually stalking her. Darren has a thing for blue-

eyed blondes, and she happened to be one. When I spoke to her she was moving away to Florida, and her advice to me was "to get rid of him". Being as "dumb as a box of rocks," I didn't heed her advice.

I was going off to a Powwow, which is a Native American Gathering, and got up enough nerve to ask Darren if he wanted to go. He said yes. I thought this would be my chance to prove that I could snatch him back from all these women he was running with. Yeah, right. We slept in the same tent together, but I couldn't get him to do anything. One morning when he was out of the tent, I decided to go snooping in his belongings. I found nothing in his pockets, but hit pay dirt when I looked inside his "medicine bag". Let me explain. A medicine bag is a person's personal thing. They put things in there that hold special meaning for them and no one is supposed to touch it or look inside. Well, let me tell you, I didn't care. I carefully opened it, and was shocked by what I found. There were tiny little ribbons that came off women's bras. There was a hunk of red hair tied with a ribbon, along with an earring, and a woman's watch. I almost puked. I couldn't believe it! This wasn't a medicine bag! It was a bag meant to attract the woman of your dreams. This was what the so-called medicine man was teaching him. I put the stuff back the way I had found it, and never said a thing. Later that day Darren and I were walking around the powwow grounds when we ran into a mutual friend. The friend looked at us both with a weird expression on his face. I later found out that this friend had seen Darren with a real young blue- eyed blonde, and he was shocked to see us together.

You are not going to believe this, but it is now February, in the year 2002, and I am just now getting back to the writing of this book. And to think, I started it in January 2000! I guess I am suffering from something called "writer's block". Anyway, let's get back to the story. This part is Jerry Springer quality.

Darren had decided to go to a trade school while living his new life. Because he couldn't drive, he would have to take a bus. While riding the bus, he met a woman that was the biggest nut case on the planet. She loved Indians, and she wanted Darren. She zeroed in on him and went to town. It seems that she was a recovering addict also, except she didn't go to AA. She didn't believe in it. She also didn't believe Darren should be taking his prescribed medicine either, so she made him stop, and he did. She told him that AA and his medication were just crutches. She was into magic and sex, and she used it for all it was worth. Me being a private investigator wannabe, was able to keep track of most of Darren's movements.

Michelle, and I were dying to see what this woman looked like, and Michelle decided to go to the woman's house. It was an action totally out of the blue. Michelle was out driving around, and called me *from a pay phone and told me what she was going to do. When she came home, she said," It's all about sex and control, and she is a" skank"). That was it. To me a "skank" is a skinny, nasty woman that will do anything sexually. YUK! Of course it is my opinion, and you know what they say about opinions.*

I had found several letters that the "skank" had written to him. They were very childish. One of them was a drawing of a stick man and a stick woman lying side by side in bed together. The head of the bed had a heart drawn into it. That wasn't what made the picture. It was where the stick figures had their hands. On each other's crotches, and the note beneath it read; "I like it much better like this". I thought that the writer was sixteen or younger.

There was also another letter where she told Darren that his dead grandmother would appear to her, and they would converse. And he believed her! And one time they must have had an argument and he stalked off leaving her with her thoughts. She had written him a letter about this argument, begging his forgiveness. In the letter she said that she felt as if the bear was ripping her heart out, and that the eagle was pecking at her soul. And that she wanted for the both of them to go to the place where the spirit of their aborted child was, and talk things over. As I am reading this tripe, I am thinking that the writer is about sixteen years old, and living in one hell of a twisted fantasy world. I cannot believe that this is the same woman my husband is shacking up with! In case you are wondering how I happened to come by these letters, I will tell you. When he came to the house to visit our granddaughter he carried the letters in his backpack, and when he was busy and distracted, I would go through his belongings, find them, read them, and take them.

While all this crap was going on I tried to tell his probation officer what was happening, and how this woman was not conducive to Darren's better mental health, or his recovery. His PO didn't care. So Darren continued to have the time of a sixteen year old.

My daughter and I decided to set a trap, to have her call me. We did, and I taped our five- hour conversation. I couldn't believe that the woman I talked to on the phone, and the one that wrote the letters, were one and the same. I wish that there were some way that you could have heard the conversation that I had with this psycho. Just to give you an idea of the kind of twisted power that this woman had, I have to recount this specific incident. This woman became pregnant by my husband. Together they made a decision not to have the baby, and the girlfriend would have an abortion, which she did, with my husband holding her hand every step of the way. (And when I gave birth to our daughter he was home nursing a hangover, and as usual I was alone). And then, she managed to talk him into having a vasectomy. Now, here is where it gets good. This "skank" has my husband go to a Clan Mother and tell her that I did witchcraft and *caused them to lose their baby! And he did! Him, who would never go to a clan mother for anything! And him, who would never lie to a Clan Mother! And him, who knew that he was telling a bald face lie! Forget the power of cheese! This was the power of sex at work here! I got this information from my sister-in-law. She called me one day and asked me what was going on with me, and her brother, and then I asked her why she wanted to know. And then I got the story. It seems that The Clan Mother called my sister-in-law to tell her what was going on, and one thing just lead to another. Well, I wasn't going to sit still for this one! I got on the phone and called a friend and told her what had transpired. She told me that she would call me back, and she did. She had set up an appointment for that evening with a medicine woman who would help me out with this dilemma. Tradition dictates that when a medicine woman, man, or seer helps you out with a problem, you in turn give them a token. It can be in the form of money, food, anything, even a candy bar. Well, I didn't have any money, but this woman sure did get a few of my best ceramic creations for her efforts. I did basically everything she asked me to do. I believed in her until one evening she, my daughter, and I, were sitting around discussing the "skank". My daughter just happened to mention that her father owed me a lot for the many years that we had been together, and for all the caring things that I had done for him. Well, the Medicine Woman pipes up and says that he didn't owe me anything, however, he did owe the "skank". Right then and* there I knew that she knew the "skank", and then I figured she was a fraud. That was the last time that I ever had the wool pulled over my eyes. There are many Medicine people in this world, however, very few are real, and the faker's thrive on the stupidity and ignorance of others. This was one of the major lessons I learned at this point in my life. Oh, I'm still as "dumb as a box of rocks," but now the rocks are being reduced to pebbles. (I think.)

You are not going to believe this, but I have been away from the writing of this book for a long time. It is now 2003, and nothing much has changed. Same crap, different day. Can you believe it? When I look back at my life, I wonder what in hell was it all about? Why did I want to stay married to this man? What was it that I was lacking in my life, that I would subject myself to such emotional pain and trauma? And how could I react the way that I did to my husband's indiscretions? What did I ever do in this life that was so horrible, that I would tolerate such abuse? As many times as I have pondered that question, I still cannot come up with an answer. If I were a believer in Karma, I would say that in my other life I had been very rich, and spoiled. I was a real mean bitch, and never shared or cared about anyone. That makes more sense to me than anything else I can come up with.

Darren ended up leaving the "skank" and getting an apartment of his own. He didn't like living there by himself so he started to come around home, more and more. Before I knew it, he was back in my life again. And I let him. I kept hearing my sister's voice over and over in my head. "Be careful of what you pray for, you just might get it." And now I know the real meaning of those words. He was still the same arrogant, selfish, self centered, egotistical jackass that he always was. He still got drunk, and high on weed, but he no longer chased women. He would just leer at them like he was an old letch. Now there are two grandchildren. One girl, and one boy. You can say anything you want about this man, but he does love his grandchildren. For them, he would give his life, and they adore him too. He doesn't get plastered in front of them, and seldom even gets drunk, and I believe that it is because of them, and he doesn't want them to grow up like my boy's, and our daughter.

The four remaining children from my first marriage have all grown up and gone their own way. Ryan married his high school sweetheart, and had three girls. His wife is a real sweetheart. He worked various jobs, and did construction on the side. His wife also worked. He and his wife bought a home with a in-ground pool. After a year or two they added on to the house, and it was beautiful. I used to say that Ryan liked to live the lifestyle of the rich and unfamous.

After umpteen years of marriage he left his wife and daughter's to take up with what I call a "skank". Ryan told his wife that the reason he left her was *because she never cooked him breakfast in the nude. Can you believe that? What in hell was going on in his mind? When you have children you can't play out your fantasies with them under foot. Needless to say, Ryan left this "skank" for another one. They had a baby girl together. I understand through the grapevine that their relationship is one of violence. They knock each other around. I have never met her, and don't care to. I don't see much of Ryan either. I just can't get beyond what he did to his wife. I am still friends with his ex wife, and she is like a daughter to me even though we don't see each other very often. Like every other man that leaves his wife, he blames her and say's that he wasn't happy. Well, when we used to go to his house in the summer for cookouts he sure as hell looked and acted happy to me. Ryan is too handsome for his own good. My children may be my children, but when they are wrong, they are wrong, and I will not take their side when they are. I call it like I see it, much to their chagrin.*

Now, about my son Travis; He grew up and raced motorcycles, just like his father, and he was good at it. He was also a terrific businessman, and had his own construction company. He married an older woman who was very nice. Her name is June. In the beginning, before I got to know her, I asked him why he didn't find a woman closer to his own age. He said, that no one could take care of him as good as she could. He said that no one would cook, clean, wait on him hand and foot, give him everything, and work as hard as she did. And he was right, no woman in this day and age would.

Travis and his wife took me to Colorado with them. All my kid's chipped in and gave me spending money, and Travis paid for my plane fare, and room. They all knew that I needed a vacation really bad as I had been going through hell with Darren, and at this time he was in another rehab program. And oh, what a wonderful adventure it was!

Up until this trip I had been reading some books written by Mary Summer Rain. All of her stories were based in Colorado, and all the while I read, the more I dreamed of Colorado. I fell in love with the state through reading the books, and never dreamed that I would actually go there, and then budda bing budda boom! I was on my way. This was the first time. When I returned home I felt as if I had left the land of my birth behind, and I wanted to go back there to live. I do believe that I was depressed for two weeks after my return.

Once again two years later my son Travis, and his wife June took me to Colorado again, and this time we went to New Mexico. I was like a kid at Christmas, and my head was on the move continuously. I was always exclaiming, oh my God! Oh my God! Look at that! You would think I had never been there before. Unless you have been there it is very difficult to explain the beauty of these two states. They are unlike anything else you have ever seen. I could have spent the rest of my life wandering through these states, and never get bored. I remembered telling my son to get me a horse, bedroll, and a rifle, and turn me loose. He would just laugh. The sad thing was that I had to go back home, and I hated it. Oh yeah...reality.

One more opportunity arose for me to get back to Colorado, and New Mexico. My husband and I were members of a committee that had to go to a national conference, and it was being held at the University of New Mexico. This time my husband went. The committee had a fund-raiser that paid his way. He had to stay in the dorm at the University, and I stayed with my sister at a hotel just outside of Albuquerque. She and I had a rental car so that we could go back and forth to the campus. When the conference was over we put my husband on a plane and sent him back home. We were going on to Colorado, and we couldn't afford to have him along.

For a week my sister and I traveled all over Colorado, and New Mexico. When we were in Farmington, New Mexico, I wanted to ride out on what seemed like the desert, so that I could actually put my hands on Shiprock. I had to settle for looking at it through binoculars because my sister was too afraid to take the rental over the dirt roads that we would have needed to take to get to it. If I were the one that had rented it, I would have said "dirt roads be damned, and full speed ahead." Actually, I paid for half of the rental, but she was the one that used her credit card to get the car, so I couldn't force the issue.

My sister had a girlfriend who owned some property in Colorado, but she had never seen it. When she heard that Kate was going to be in Colorado, she gave her the map of the property so that we could look for it and take pictures of the place. Well, let me tell you, we found it all right, in no man's land.

There was a main office with a huge map on the wall filled with different colored pins. Each color denoted a particular piece of property, and where, hopefully you could find it. It seems that people were buying parcels of land, so that when they retired from their careers they could move there, and build their dream home. Until such time you could live in a mobile home while you were in the process of building. Kate and I took off and started looking. We did see a trailer or two, now and then, and then there was nothing except wilderness, and more wilderness. It was absolutely breathtaking in it's desolate beauty. It seemed as though we had driven a hundred miles before we actually found the property. We finally stopped, and got out of the car, and walked around. What was once a white car, was now light tan with dust. I swear, it was so quiet that you could hear the blood pumping through your arteries. This is definitely not a place for a heart attack or a broken bone. Rescue would have been too late. After we took pictures we decided to leave as night was approaching, and we didn't want to be there in the dark. My sister let me drive, and I put the pedal to the metal, and virtually flew out of there. Needless to say, we didn't go out the way we had gone in, but we did manage to make it to a major highway, which was almost devoid of any traffic. When we got on the road, my sister took over the driving. She was tired of bouncing around like popcorn in a popper, and we didn't even know where we were. I told her that we were not lost, but on an adventure. Eventually we came to a small town, and got a room for the night. Kate, and I had a great time. We put over two thousand miles on that rental, and a few pounds on our hips from all the junk food we consumed along the way. And then the fun was over, and we had to take the plane back to reality, and the "stone quarry."

I say "stone quarry," because that box of rocks that had turned into pebbles had soon morphed back in to rocks. Even though Darren had been on the spiritual retreat in New Mexico, it wasn't too long before he was back into the drinking, and still smoking dope, and I was back to the sleepless nights, and the worrying, and the panic attacks that come with it. I forgot to mention that at this time our daughter, her husband, and their baby girl had moved into my house, and I had remodeled a large room at the back of my garage into a mini apartment, and this was where I was living when Darren returned. There was no shower, or bathroom. We had to go into the main house to take care of our hygienic needs. This was a real pain in the tuckus, as it caused many problems between my son-in-law, our daughter, and me. I *would feel that she wasn't taking proper care of my house, so I would complain. I also didn't like the way her husband treated my granddaughter. He wouldn't let her do anything unless he was right there to watch her. He was over protective, and of course, I couldn't keep my mouth shut. He was also a lazy slob, and that really irritated me. One day I had a battle with my daughter, and they moved out into an apartment. It wasn't too long before they had to move back into my house, and Darren and I moved back out to "the room," better known as "the little house."*

I have digressed, and need to get back to my adult children. I had been talking about my son Travis and his wife June. I was not aware that Travis had a drug problem. I knew he smoked pot once in awhile, but I didn't know about the crack. Not until the time his wife called and told me that he had a problem, and that he needed help. I went over to his house, and discussed it with him. I made up my mind to go to work with him for two weeks, and sit with him at night until his wife came home for work. He went along with this, and I thought that he had gotten over the hump, and could do the rest himself so I stopped going over to his house. God! Just how dumb can one person be? You would have thought that I would have learned from my husband's alcoholism, but I didn't. Crack is not like alcohol. It is far worse. I found out the crack had him by the ass on a down hill grade, and he is out of control. His business was going to hell, along with his marriage. The next thing you know he left his wife for another woman. June could no longer afford to stay in the house because she had been injured on her job, so she moved out, and in with her daughter. I felt so bad for his wife because she worked so hard for him, and she really did love him in spite of the age difference.

June and I are still friends to this day. It has been three years this past May, and I still hear about what he did to her, and how he did the crack, and what he did to feed his habit. This is very, very sad, because he really is a nice guy. The first Christmas with his girlfriend he came to the family Christmas party and brought his new girlfriend, Janeen. She was about his age and, she seemed to be very nice. I asked her if she knew he had a drug problem, and she said yes, that she was trying to help him. In my heart I wanted it to be so. The next Christmas she told me that she didn't baby him or wait on him hand, and foot, like his first wife did. I thought that this was a good thing. Oh, and Travis never fathered any children that we know of.

My daughter Jamie graduated from college, married a teacher, had a baby boy, and had her own business for a while. She gave up the business because she was going to have another baby, however it had been at least five years since she had her first son. They own, and live in a beautiful home in the country with an in-ground pool. Both children are engaged in a sport of some kind. They do things together as a family, and you know that the children are truly loved by their parents. My daughter seems to be happier than a pig in poop.

Now, my son Matthew is a story. As a boy growing up with his father, and being subjected to his father's many wives, and their temperaments, and Lord knows what-all turned out different than his brothers who like to do all the manly things like hunting, fishing motorcycling, and chasing women. He was more gentle, and feminine, but managed to go into the construction business, and did well for himself. He had three wives, and ended up divorcing them. He had no children. He lived with two women who were real beauts, especially the last one. She was into witchcraft, and weird. One Halloween she brought out the feminine side of Matthew. She painted him up, and dressed him like a woman. He looked like a hooker on crack. This was the beginning of the morphing of my son, into my daughter. He became a trans-sexual, and was a man by day, and a woman by night. The next thing I know my son is having implants and has taken on a feminine name. I was a little upset, but was able to understand his predicament. He had explained to me that he always felt like a girl, and never wanted to do manly things. He now wanted to have an operation that would turn him into a "real" woman. He couldn't have the procedure done here in the United States, so he and another trans-sexual flew to Thailand, and had the transforming surgery done there. They went as men, and came back as women. The one thing that I am having a problem understanding is, why would you want to be a female if you still liked girls? The men in her life seem to be just sugar daddies. She has her own business in Louisiana as a masseuse, and seems to be doing well. She is happy, hurts no one, and uses no one, and I guess that is all that counts. It is definitely a different world today. If you don't like your gender, you can change it. You can change anything. Not me though. The only thing I want to change is my address. I have lived in my house for twenty-two years. I have been here too long, besides, there is a dark cloud that hangs over this house like a shroud. It is time for change. Change is good. Moving is good. Getting up the courage to make the move...well, that is a different story all together.

As this story moves on we come to my son Luke. He is a good man also. He is married to a sweet woman, and they have four children. They both work very hard. He during the day, and she in the evening, and Luke baby sits. They own their own home. One humongous problem. My son is a pill-head. He is addicted to pain killers, and when he can't get them I have heard that he uses heroin, and once in awhile crack. I don't know whether this is true or not, but I suspect that it is. He is now missing work, and is behind in his bills, and he makes way too much money to be late paying for anything. His wife works three part time jobs to help out. I really feel sorry for her. I think she loves him too much. She shouldn't even have to work outside the home. With four children, and two of them babies, and the housework, I feel that is *enough work for a tiny woman like her. Whenever I see him, I am on him constantly about his addictions. (the pills) I try to explain that one day he will keel over dead from them. I even point out how much his wife, and children need him. It doesn't matter. The pills seem to be the only thing that matters. And that is sad because he is really a great dad, and loves his kid's. He interacts with them, and shows them how much he loves them. He borrows money from me every month. Of course he pays me back, but that isn't the point. He shouldn't have to borrow money. I told him the last time he borrowed money that I was afraid I wouldn't get it back when he dropped dead. He just pooh poohs me.*

And now for the life of Storm, He seems to have lived up to his name. Another one. Nice home in the suburbs, nice, over understanding wife, that works, and three children. He is a good father, and a good provider. He is also very strict with them. He is an alcoholic. Before she went to work many years ago she would call me, and ask for my advice. Of course, I probably gave her the wrong information because I didn't want the family to break up, and they didn't. It wasn't until she got out into the workforce that she began to change. I have to admit that it was for the better. She could now be somewhat independent, and not rely on him for everything. His wife and children left him once because he was so violent, and disgusting when he was drunk. My son treated her like crap, and she is a hard worker, and a good mother.

My son kept begging, pleading, and promising that if she would just come back home that he would be the kind of guy that she had always wanted. Oh, and he worked at it with a vengeance. He sent flowers, candy, rubbed her feet when he went to visit the children, and yup! He suckered her right back into the same old crap, except he isn't quite as bad as he used to be. The problem with this son, was that almost every night he would call me and tell me how much his family meant to him, and how much he loved his wife. I tried to tell him that it is the drinking that is causing his problems. He said he knew, but that he would stop if she would just take him back, and give him another chance. Why, hell! I even believed him! Me, who has spent the last thirty years with an alcoholic. He is now drinking as much as ever, and I fear that his wife will leave him for good this time. Quite frankly, I wouldn't blame her. She and the kid's have put up with far too much of his crap too.

When Storm was twenty-one he finally went to Virginia to meet his father. Of course his father said that he couldn't be sure that Storm was his son. The jerk even told him that I had slept with his business partner. That was a bald-faced lie. I never did. Funny thing about me, when I was having an affair, it was only with one man at a time. His daughters, who are my son's half sister's said that he looks, and sounds exactly like their father, and guess what? That jerk is a drunk too. His wife has been through her own hell with this man, but refuses to leave him because they are Catholics.

I come now to my youngest daughter Michelle. She hooked up with that idiot that I wrote about earlier. She met him when she was working at the mall. The next thing I knew they wanted to move to Maine together. I was not happy with this at all, and expressed my feelings about it. As usual, no one was listening. Well, maybe listening, but not paying attention. When I realized that I couldn't talk them out of it, I told her boyfriend, the idiot, that he had better take care of her, and not let anything bad happen to her. He promised that he would, and away they went.

About a month or two later they were back. They moved in with his parents, and the next thing you know, she is pregnant! I am not happy because of the idiot father. She gave birth to a daughter, and was a good mother. They moved into a nice apartment, and were happy until the idiot was hurt on the job, and then her happy life turned into a nightmare. They ended up having to move into my house because now there was no money. They got their food from a local food pantry, and his parents paid two hundred dollars a month for them to live in my house. They also paid all of his bills. Again I had a big fight with the two of them. They moved out into another apartment with the help of his family. I almost forgot. During this time I found out that they were married. It was by accident. I was shocked, and pissed off, all at the same time, but there was nothing I could do about it. As far as I was concerned, the damage had been done.

Five years later Michelle becomes pregnant again, and has a boy. Things for her are becoming worse. Her now husband is on the phone every day whining to the doctors and the compensation board about his back injury. He never lets up, and hearing him whine day after day was beginning to wear on Michelle. She went and found herself a job, and left him to take care of the baby boy. The girl was in kindergarten, so he only had to deal with the baby, and you already know what happened there.

Michelle, being three quarters American Indian, was becoming interested in the Indian Culture. (her father, my husband is full blooded, and I am one quarter Indian). Me, and my sister Kate had been doing American Indian Ceramics and we had a booth at a few Powwows, which are a gathering of native people that share their culture through dancing, and artwork. One weekend Michelle came to one, and brought the two kids. She fell in love with the dancing, and the camaraderie of the vendors, and the people. She decided that she wanted to be a dancer, and so did her daughter. The following year she went to the Powwows, brought the children, and eventually became a head dancer. Her husband was not happy at this turn of events. He didn't really like Indians, even though he married one. He tried to stop her from going and taking the children with her. He even went as far as to call the police. They came, and told him he didn't have a leg to stand on, because the powwow was a part of her culture, she was the children's natural mother, and that was that. He was livid. After that powwow she came back home, and moved into the main house, and her father and I were back into "the room, known as the little house."

Michelle went to work as a barmaid, and earned good money, and we babysat for her. She made great tips because she has a winsome personality with strangers. After about a month she met Harrison. He was divorced, older, and came from an affluent family. You would have never known it by his actions. He had just come out of a relationship where he lost everything he had. He was also a boozer, and a crack head. I didn't have a clue in the beginning. He could charm the undies off a Nun. Michelle started to fall into the same trap I did, and I couldn't stop her. He moved in with her and her children. A month hadn't passed when I had to lock horns with him. In other words, we had an explosive argument, which I won. After the argument things settled down somewhat. And then Bam! One night while they were sleeping Harrison had a grand mal seizure. Michelle came running out to ask me to stay with the kids while he went to the hospital. He had never had a seizure before. I think it was a combination of a previous head injury and the crack. The doctor asked him if he did drugs. He was honest and answered yes. Because of the seizure he could no longer do the crack, and on top of it he was remanded to probation on a DWI. Michelle thought that things were looking up. There was just one big problem. He could no longer do the type of work that he had been doing, so he did odd jobs for a while.

This was not enough money to make ends meet. Michelle couldn't work because of her back problem, and her migraines kicked in, and she lost her job. So now things really start to go bad. One day they were fighting when I went into the house, and I suggested that I take him to his brothers house. She told me to get out and mind my own business. I left and went outside. Harrison came out and asked me to take him to his brothers. I did. Well, Michelle came flying out of the house. She slammed the door so hard that she broke the door panel. She also called me a cunt. Can you believe that? Now I am pissed off at both of them, but as usual I got over it real quick. Along my busted up road of life I learned that it is easier to let go of anger, and hatred, and roll with the punches that life deals out because if you don't, it will make you a sick and vicious person. I don't ever want to be like that.

Harrison is working his A.A. program with a vengeance, and he is beginning to change. I told Michelle that he would, because once he stopped drinking and drugging, the real Harrison would show up, and he was a selfish, self-centered jerk. All he cared about was himself and his sobriety. The more things went bad, the more they would fight and argue. One night *she threw a small safe at him, and it missed and hit the bedroom wall. The arguing was so bad, and loud that one of the neighbors called the police. I was mortified. I don't like having the police coming to my house. Most of the time when they fought the kids were at their father's, or in my "little house" so they weren't exposed to the violence. An opportunity arose for Harrison to leave. It was only supposed to be temporary, but the relationship ended. Thank God. About four months after Harrison was gone, so were her migraines. What does that tell you?*

Six months later Michelle met another guy. His name is Steven. This one seems to be nice, and a hard worker. He has never been married and has no children. He bought her a nice diamond ring, and proposed to her. Unlike her last boyfriend, this one is involved with the children. They all eat dinner together at the dining room table, and they do things together as a family. They are looking for a three-bedroom home in the country where the kids can have pets. Right now there isn't enough room in my house. There are only two bedrooms, and I worry that the kids will become "Jerry Springer" close. The kids like Steven, and that is important. Myself, I like him too, but am taking a wait and see attitude. Darren...he doesn't have an opinion, and if he does he doesn't vocalize.

I am still with Darren, and it has been thirty years. Thirty long, hard, years. He doesn't drink or get drunk like he used to. How long it will last? I don't know. What will I do if he starts doing it again? I don't know. There was a time when it was every weekend. Now it is down to twice a year. He still drinks his beer, but doesn't get drunk. And guess what? He doesn't get plastered on Christmas or New Years Eve anymore. I'm not holding my breath.

Darren is now a diabetic, and impotent. It doesn't bother me that we can't have sex, as I am no longer the sexy babe that he married. I wouldn't even want to have sex with me, if I were him. He doesn't work, because he isn't capable of communicating. I mean, he can talk, but he can't get his point across in an intelligent manner. He doesn't have pride in his looks anymore, and he no longer uses his manners, whether at home, or in public. If he has to pass gas, belch, or feels the need to pick his nose, he does. He just doesn't care anymore, and the VA thinks that he is okay.

His Post Traumatic Syndrome has taken its toll on his abilities to function in a productive manner. We have been fighting with the Veteran's Administration for his service-connected pension. They have him at thirty percent, when he should be at a hundred percent disabled. They say that he was in PTS before he joined the Marines, and went to Vietnam. He only gets $135.00 a month from the VA. They are now going to take thirty of that a month for medication that he has been getting for the PTSD that he didn't get from the war. Talk about getting screwed, blued, and tattooed. It has happened to him because of the war, and the VA, and it has happened *to me because I married, and hung in there with him. We exist on $1,152.00 a month. Our mortgage is $533.00 a month. By the time I pay our bills we are left with $140.00 a month for groceries, and gas. My income is from Workmen's compensation, and Social Security disability. When my daughter, her fiancée, and the kid's move out, we will have to pay $150.00 a month for utilities. Somehow I will manage. I always do.*

Just to give you a little look at my husband's lack of civility. Two years ago he and I took a trip to Pennsylvania to a Black Powder Shoot. We took a tent and sleeping bags along, and camped in a state park. He would sit right on the picnic table and smoke dope, and he would take a leak, (relieve himself) right where he could be seen if someone should happen to look our way. Why, he even went to another camper, a stranger, and asked the guy if he had a beer, and last but not least he would just let rip with a round of gas, and didn't care that it could wipe out all the wildlife in the area.

Every now, and then if he gets plastered, he will take a leak right out in the driveway. Of course it is dark out, but we do have neighbors. He also relieves himself in the side yard, even when he isn't drinking, of course, it's dark out but that isn't the point. When I call him on it, he will say that no one cares, and I answer back with," I do."

It doesn't matter how I feel about anything. He will do what he wants to do, and every one else be damned. But the VA says there is nothing wrong with him, and I say, that they don't live with him on a day, to day basis. After just one session with a psychiatrist, they loaded him up with meds, and never followed up. The only medication he takes on a daily basis is one that helps him to sleep through the night. He walks around making weird little clicking sounds, or walking in a weird fashion. Sometimes I think he gets his kicks by pissing everybody off.

Darren had a temporary job at the VA as part of a rehab program. He worked outside on building and grounds maintenance. It was only for six months, and he almost had an extension, but ended up quitting.

Below you can read a letter that I wrote to his Purple Heart Rep at the VA. It was after his last horrible drunk and I wanted them to know that he really has a problem. However, I never sent it. I don't know why, maybe, because it is so horrible, and I would be humiliated because I know his rep. A few lines may seem familiar, because I had already mentioned them, but this is on a larger scale.

Dear Ms. Smithers,
I am writing to you because I don't know who else to turn to at the VA. Darren is no better now than he was before. If anything he is worse. He had opted to extend his position as groundskeeper until the end of October, which would have been a great help

to us financially. Well, last Tuesday he went to work, and was back home by eleven thirty and swilling Irish Creme. When I asked him what he was doing home so early, and why was he drinking, he said because he didn't want to clean under the dumpsters anymore because the stench made him gag. And that was it!

Now, he spends his time drinking beer and smoking marijuana. He leaves the house and never says where he is going. I never know where he is. He is like Pan, Laughing and dancing through life without a care or a responsibility. The only thing he cares for on this planet are his grandchildren. He interacts with them, not as a grandfather, but at their age level because he is high most of the time. Our grandchildren have not made the connection between drunk, and drinking beer. They do however know that he smokes dope. When they tell me that he is doing that, all I can tell them is that he is smoking Indian Tobacco. This will sound gross, but he prefers to urinate outside up against the fence adjoining my neighbor's yard, against my Japanese Cherry tree ,or in my Climatis that grow in the corner of the yard. Last summer we went on a camping trip to Pennsylvania. We camped in a State Park While we were there he sat on the picnic table and smoked pot, and he would urinate out in the open, where he could possibly be seen. Again, I asked him to please not do those things where he could be seen. His answer was," What do I care? I will never see these people again". I tried to explain to him that these actions repulse people, and by acting in that fashion he is probably ruining

any opportunity of meeting, and making new friends.
He didn't care. I don't go to many places with him
anymore because his behavior is reprehensible. He
thinks nothing of passing gas, or belching out loud
in public.

I am not even sure if you are aware that last Fall
he was arrested for shoplifting at our local grocery
store here in town and it wasn't the first time. I
caught him once putting a brick of cheese into his
pocket, and I made him put it back, and then I went
off to do more shopping. On the way home he pulled
out the cheese, and started eating it. I couldn't
believe he did that. However, once he was arrested,
he never did it again, and said that he didn't even
know why he ever shoplifted to begin with!

I have no control over Darren or what he does,
nor do I want to control him. He does whatever he
wants to, when he wants to. It seems that the more
programs he tries, the worse he becomes. We have
been married for thirty years, and for thirty years
I have watched him steadily decline. Darren is not a
bad man. He isn't even a mean man, he is just a very
sick man. Won't you please help?

Sincerely,
Mesa Morgan

I have spent thirty years hoping, and praying that
something, or someone would help him to get well. He
has no pride or self esteem. While he was working

at the hospital some of his self esteem returned.
I believed he actually liked his job. Sometimes he
would come home all excited about going to school
for some type of training, and then the next thing I
knew, he was no longer thinking about school or any
other self improvements. He drives my sister Kate
crazy. He will walk in her house, and if there is food
out, he will just up, and help himself without asking.
He does the same thing with our daughter. That is so
rude, however he does take care of the yard, baby-
sit, take out the trash, and keep my vehicle running
so he isn't all bad. That is a great help because I
couldn't do that for myself not with these aching
bones, and especially not with a broken foot. The
reason I have a broken foot is because I fell off my
sexy shoes. I have these neat sandals that my sister
bought me. They only have a band of leather that
goes across your instep, but the heel is about three
inches high. I like them because they added height
to my short, fat self, and they were lightweight so
I could move fast in them. Well, one day I was out
planting silk flowers into the white swan planter on
my front porch when I stepped backward. All of a
sudden, bam! Down I went. Normally I would have
sworn like a muleskinner but I didn't make a sound
because I had seen the woman across the street
was outside in her yard. This even made it worse.
She came across the street, and asked me if I was
all right, and did I break my foot? I said no, and
then I said no when she wanted to help me up. She
looked at my feet and said, "it was the shoes", I
looked at her feet, and said, "yeah, they are just

like yours", except hers had straps around the ankle. She finally left, and took off in her car. I was waving as she drove away, and then I got up. I didn't think anything was broken until I kept walking, and the more I walked, the worse the pain became. I finally got into my truck, and drove to the emergency room, and told them that I thought I broke my foot, and showed them where I thought it was broke. They took an x-ray, and told me that it was broken exactly where I told them. I had to wait until the next day to get a cast, and the thing went up to my knee. I wouldn't let it keep me down, and in one week I had worn a hole in the heel, and the rest of the bottom looked like a well worn tire. I had to go and have it recast, and then two weeks later I went to have it removed, but now have to wear a funny shoe for three more weeks, and me with a ton of things that need doing!

There is another medical episode I need to tell you about. Last July 2002, I had to have emergency surgery. I was shocked! The night before I went to the emergency room I had been eating pizza, and felt fine. At about ten thirty pm, I started to have sharp pain across my abdomen, and then I started to barf uncontrollably. This went on until three in the morning. I felt as if I was going to pass out so I called 911 and asked for an ambulance. I had to tell them what was wrong before they would send one, and then I told them, no lights, and siren. I went out and sat on the front stoop, and waited for them. Everyone was sound asleep, and never knew I had left. The next morning I called from the hospital to let my daughter know where I was, and what had happened. At first the doctors thought that I could have elective surgery, but after an MRI it had turned into emergency surgery. It seemed that my stomach had somehow fallen into my intestines, and the intestine was being choked off. They came to me in my drugged up state and told me that they might have to give me a colostomy. I just sort of sat up, and told them that no matter what, to try, and not do that because I didn't have time to deal with a bag. As it turned out, I had eight hernias. They repaired them, and everything turned out ok. Seven days after I left the hospital I had to go back and have the staples removed. I asked the doctor if I was cleared for take off, as I had to leave for vacation the next day. He said, no, not for six to eight weeks. I was like WHAT? He explained why I couldn't drive or go on a long ride. I just said ok, and left. The next day I was on my way. I had a body pillow stuffed around me, and I hit the road. When I finally reached my destination I needed my pain meds, and a good rest. The next day I felt much better. I know, me, and I know what my limits are, and some times I feel like wonder woman. Maybe that is why I am still here, and kicking. That, and I am on this planet for a reason, but I have yet to figure out what the reason is.

I plan on living to be a hundred. I have too many places to go, and too many things to see, and experience. Even though I feel that my life has been hell, I have been happy at times, because of the things around, above, and below me. The trees, the flowers, the birds, and wildlife. A sunrise, a sunset. The four seasons, and most of all, Christmas. Not for the gifts, but for the spirit, and the way it makes me feel.

I am a sky person, and can spend hours just looking at the night sky, pondering the mystery of it, especially in the summer, however, I have to fight the mosquitoes off to do it. These are simple things, and cost no money, but they sure put a smile in my heart. Oh my! I am rambling on so. I had better get back to the story.

My sister Kate lives behind me across the yard with her boyfriend Alex of twenty-five years or more. He is my husband's brother, but they are as different as day, and night. He doesn't drink, and has always worked. My sister has a great job with the federal government. Her two boys are grown, but not married. Lucky her. David has grown into a nice quiet young man who loves his solitude. He is an introvert. However, his brother Troy is just the opposite. High energy, with an in your face attitude, and is always busy doing something. Kate is pretty much happy with her life. She and I do a lot together. We shop, we do ceramics, and we watch TV, and sometimes we sit, and try to solve the problems of the world. My sister, and my brother-in-law have helped us on, and off over the years. I never ask them for anything except to borrow coffee, an onion, or some little *thing that I may need to use in cooking. If they offer, I accept, but not willingly. If I borrow money, I always pay it back.*

My brother Bill had a great job making great money. He married a woman that knew how to keep him happy. She just fed him. A lot. They had a boy and a girl. His wife worked also, so they never knew what it was like to want, or need anything, and neither did their children. For years they lived close by, and then when their kid's grew up, they retired, sold everything, including the house, bought an RV and took off to see America. They traded that in for a fifth-wheeler that has an extended living room. I haven't seen it, but I can just imagine how it looks. Once my brother married we stopped being close for whatever reason. I saw him and his wife last year at a family picnic, and that is how we heard of the change in their lives. I know they are on the road somewhere, and I have e-mailed them once, but they never responded.

About my sister Edith, When she was young she married and divorced her first husband because he was a drunk. She has two boys. They seem to be great kids, but I only get to see them every two years or so. She played the field for a long time and then she met the man who would become her second husband. He was from a wealthy family. She had a beautiful Fairy Tale wedding, and then she and her husband moved to California. He was a successful boat salesman, and she owns her own real estate business. She has all the money she could ever need or want. She and her husband live in a seventeen-room house in a gated community with an in-door pool that has a waterfall. And guess what? She wants an even bigger house. Can you imagine that? They have all the toys, and live the "good" life. I am not jealous because she busted her butt to get where she is, and so did her husband. You know what is amusing here? Both my brother Bill and my sister Edith were illegitimate, but somehow they overcame that to lead successful happy lives. Me, my sister Kate, and my brother Joey all had the same father, and the only successful one out of we three was Kate. Joe died on the streets of San Francisco after he came back from Vietnam. He just couldn't deal with his demons, and became a street person. And I am a writer, and a poet. I have never made any money at it, even though I am very good at what I do. I have a small portfolio of my published editorials, and one with my poems. I am also the only one of us that graduated college with a degree, and managed to make the Dean's list three times out of four. Of course, it didn't help me much, as my disability became worse just before I graduated. I have since regained most of my mobility, but now just seem to be too old for employment, however, I haven't given up, and I am still wishing, and hoping. I know that someday something wonderful is going to happen, I just don't know where, when, or what. I have several grandchildren, thirteen to be exact, and two great grand children. One born while I was working on this book.

My oldest granddaughter Dawn, is the daughter of my son that was killed. He had taken her from her mother and moved to Texas. Before he was killed she was like a little mother to her dad. As small as she was she was the one that would get him up, and see that he went to work. When she came back from there, her life was very fragmented but she managed to overcome her problems. She never got into trouble like other girls from dysfunctional families seem to do. She managed to keep her wits about her and did exceptionally well in school. She graduated, and went to college. She is a sweetheart. She is definitely Mensa material. She is married to what I would refer to as a Mensa man. They have a little girl and a little boy, and the children are extremely intelligent, and gifted. She is a stay at home mom because her husband makes enough money at his profession. They own their own home, and appear to be very happy. Thank God.

My son Ryan had three children with his former wife. All were girls. The oldest daughter is graduating from high school this year, and the youngest one wants to be a veterinarian when she grows up. I think she will make a good one. Their mother has done an excellent job of raising them even though she has had to work. I never really get to see these grandchildren because they live quite far away. Well, it wouldn't be so far if I could afford the gas to get there. Ryan also has a little girl by his girlfriend. I have only had contact with her once, and it was at the last Christmas party. She is cute, but rather spirited.

My daughter Jamie is married to a professional man. They have a boy, and a girl. They are terrific kid's, and very talented in sport's. They do very well in school. I get to see them a little more often, but not much, because they live a little closer. Both of these children are little sweethearts. But, of course, they are like their mom, and let's not forget their dad. He is no slouch either.

My son Luke has two boys, and two girls. The oldest boy is very handsome, but a bit of a pain in the tuckus. His next son, is adorable with the most beautiful big brown eyes, and the longest eyelashes. Both girls are very petite, and pretty. I can't describe them much more than I have because they haven't been around long enough to have any accomplishments.

My son Storm has two boys and a girl. His daughter is very, very smart and does exceptionally well in school. So much so, that she was moved into a "gifted" class. His sons excels at sports, and are little cuties. They are all great kid's.

My daughter Michelle has a boy and a girl from her first marriage, and can have no more. Thank God. Her daughter is finally doing well in school. After the divorce she had a hard time of it. Because she lives on my property she is a great help to me, even though she sometimes irritates the hell *out of me with her lack of backbone. She is overly sensitive and very weepy at times. Of course, she is only eleven, and at that in between stage. I call her Sara Bernhardt, after the old time actress who was overly dramatic in her acting. The boy, is a cutie, and very, very intelligent. He has a way about him that makes you laugh. He is odd, but not in an adverse way. He eats no red meat, no vegetables, and only apples. He will eat, macaroni and cheese, cheese pizza, grilled cheese sandwiches, french fries, scads of yogurt, and mashed potatoes swimming in butter. And of course, all the junk food he can get. He wasn't always that way though. When he was a baby he ate every kind of baby food on the market. He was so fat that he had more rolls than a bakery. And then his mother had to go to work. His father, being a lazy lout would not open a jar of baby food, but fed him cake, cookies, candy and ice-cream all day. This went on until she left him, but by then it was too late to get the boy to change his likes, and dislikes of food. These two children are good kids also. The reason that I know so much more about these grandchildren than the others is that they are around me all the time, every day because they live in my house.*

If you have noticed, I have never used the word love when I refer to my children or grandchildren. I have always tried to show that I love them by being there for them when they need me. When they were all babies, and up until the ages of six or seven I would kiss, and hug them all the time.

It is my feeling that Love is highly over rated. The word means nothing to me. You can say how much you love someone a thousand times a day, but if you don't show it through your actions, then the word is meaningless. I watch these young teenage Rock Stars, (not on purpose) singing about love, and I am thinking...they don't have a clue. It's just a word to them. People have committed murder in the name of love.

I know that my life experiences have played a major part in the way I express my feelings, but at least I have feelings. I know, you are thinking...this woman needs a good psychiatrist. Not! By the time they finished with me, they would need one!

I have a very good friend. Her name is Olga, and we have known each other for thirty years. She and I used to say that if we ever came into money that we would help each other out. The problem is, that she came into an inheritance, and I didn't. She has sent me some money now, and then. I don't spend it on myself but use it for food, gas, vehicle repairs or something I need. Never for anything I want.   It isn't a super large amount, but it helps, and I am ashamed to accept it. I am upset because I cannot do anything for her in exchange for her generosity. My grandmother's words keep coming back to me, "If you have no pride, you have no dignity." My friend gets upset with me for feeling the way I do. She considers me her sister, and fluffs it off as family helping family. I hate charity. I have always lived by the "one hand washes the other" rule of life. I try never to take something for nothing. I am going to share with you a letter that I sent to her to thank, and explain why I get upset when she sends me money.

Hi Olga!

If you are reading this, you are back from your trip to Europe. I hope that all went well for you, and that you had a good trip. You can tell me all about it when you call. I wanted to write and thank you once again for your generosity. You can't even begin to imagine how it has helped me. For the most part, I have used the money that you have sent me for some groceries, gas, personal things like makeup, repairs on the RV, and the insurance coverage for it. I also purchased material to have an Indian dress made for my granddaughter, and a Indian shirt for my grandson when they dance at the Powwow. And for the first time in many years, (and I am not kidding,) I actually bought five pair of under wear, and a new bra for myself. I also bought Darren a pair of black sneakers for father's day as he needed them badly. The last check you sent me I am hanging on to until we leave. I have to buy propane, to run the refrigerator and stove, and fill up the RV with gas, and buy extra gas, and oil in order to run the generator to power the air conditioner, and to have a little to spend at the Powwow if at all possible.

This is going to be the last year for the RV because it is too expensive to operate, especially when we only use it three times a year. It is too old, and always needs to have something fixed. Our neighbor said that it was because it sits all year in the driveway. I just wanted you to know that I don't squander what you have sent me.

If I live to be a hundred years old I don't think I could ever repay you for your kindness. I know that we are friends but I am embarrassed about excepting money from you. Yeah...yeah... I know, that if the shoe were on the other foot I would do the same for you. There just seems to be one problem...the shoe is never on the other foot, and I am always the needy one, and at this point in time cannot reciprocate. I am the same way with my sister too. She tries to help me sometimes, and she does, but there are times when I say no, and she accepts my no. When I first started to get Social Security disability about four years ago, they gave me a lump sum of $3000.00. I went around and paid everyone that I borrowed from, and I also paid Kate back $200.00 to cover ceramic supplies that she had bought for me that previous year. She didn't want to take it, but I made her. I told her that if she didn't take the money, I wouldn't do ceramics any more or go to the powwows, and because she didn't want to do it alone she accepted. About five times a year her and Alex will take me to bingo with them. It costs Alex $100.00 to bring me along because it's big bingo at the Casino, and we also play the slots with $20.00. The first couple of times it was OK, but then when they asked me to go again, I said no because it cost too much money, and I never win. The only way they were able to get me to go again was by saying that if I won, I could give Alex half of what I won. That sounded reasonable to me. The first time I won it was $180.00. Alex's half was $90.00. I went to pay him, and he refused. He didn't want to take it. I told him that if he didn't take it that I would never go to bingo with them again. He took it, and I felt like a million bucks. Last year they took me to bingo for my birthday, and I won $200.00. When I wanted to give him half he wouldn't take it again, and again I said I wouldn't go anymore if he didn't. He said that because it was my birthday, the money was my present, and he didn't take it because he got his point across. He really, really doesn't like taking money from people, unless of course my kid's, or I borrow. Then he does, and he should, because it is money owed to him.

I have two best friends, and one good friend, and a few minor friends. You, and Patty who lives in Florida are my best friends. She is soooo poor that it is sad. Worse off than me. Of course she has mental, and physical problems to deal with, and I, thank God, don't. Well, maybe I do a little. Every so often if I can manage to, I will send her ten or twenty dollars. I wrote, and told her not to thank me, because I know exactly how she feels. Ten or twenty dollars is like a million to her. I just tell her to go have a little lunch someplace. I know it isn't much, but I know how happy she is to get it, and *it makes me feel good inside to make her happy once in awhile. I just wish that there were something tangible that I could do for you that could bring you a feel good smile. However, you do know that you can call on me for anything, and I will help if it is at all possible. You are right though, we are more like sisters, than friends, and that I shouldn't feel the way that I do when you help me. I guess that I have always looked upon any kind of help as charity, and my grandmother taught me, that to accept charity meant that I had no pride, or dignity. That is why I feel that I always must pay back for every favor or kind gesture made to me. Kate always says that the reason I am so poor is because I give everything away to someone else. For instance, when we are at a powwow, if I have made something that would make me a few good dollars, and someone really wants it but can't afford it, I will give it to them. If a stranger comes into my camp I will offer them something to eat or drink. Anyone can come to me if they have a need, and I can help. The only thing I can't offer is money because I never have any. Now isn't that a bitch? I call it following the "Golden Rule" of doing unto others. However my dear, I certainly have run on, and on haven't I? I think that this is probably the longest letter that I have ever written to anyone. :) It was something I needed to do, to explain my feelings about what you have done for me, and why I feel the way I do. Again, thanks ever so much!*

Friends always,

Mesa Morgan

Well readers, this is where I am in my life at this point in time. Getting older, poorer, and maybe, just maybe, a little wiser. Darren is still here, and I am still caring for him. Now he wants to be lovey dovey, after all these years. He is always after kisses, and hugs. And I try pushing him away, or dismissing his attempts. Sometimes he manages to sneak a kiss in, at least once a day. I ask him, "why now, after all these years?" He doesn't answer, and it has become a game between us. I told him that many years ago when I wanted hugs, and kisses he didn't deliver, so now I don't need or want them. He hasn't been drunk and stupid in a long time, and I can live with that. I think that because we have been together for so long, and been through so much, that we have become like a comfortable old pair of slippers.

I try to distance myself from everyone's problems but it doesn't work. They bring them to me. I live too close to the ones with the problems and far away from those without them. I cannot help my grown children with their personal problems because they won't listen. The ones with the addictions are the ones that cause me to worry the most. I can't imagine how they happened to turn to their drug of choice to deal with their problems. I have told them that if anyone needs to be a drunk, or have an addiction of some kind, it should be me. I raised them to be hard workers, and good fathers. I thought that they would have gotten their strength to cope with life from me, but they didn't. I understand that they grew up in a home where there was an alcoholic, but they didn't see me cave into the problems that came with that burden. I never sat on the pity pot. I never had the time. I have told them to deal with the problem, get rid of it, and then move on. The only thing you get from sitting on the pity pot is a ring around your tuckus! Most of the time I want to run away. Can you imagine? And at my age!

My dream is to someday see all the places in the world, and experience the different cultures. The Gypsy in me just wants to get moving and become the happy wanderer. Until such time that this dream comes true, I will have to be content with being an armchair traveler watching the Travel Channel.

The End

Be very careful what you pray for, you just might get it...

About the Author

The author was born in upstate New York in October of 1939

After 2 marriages and several children, the author at age 57 went to college, made the Dean's List and graduated with honors at the age of 59. Her course of study began with Journalism, and because her professor informed her that she already knew how to write, she changed her curriculum to Criminal Justice.

She writes poetry, dabbles in ceramics, and can often be found expressing her opinion in the Letters to the Editor section of her local newspaper.

Now at age 64 she hopes to be a successful writer, not just a legend in her own mind as she continues to work on that box of rocks.